Cloud-Native Development and Migration to Jakarta EE

Transform your legacy Java EE project
into a cloud-native application

Ron Veen

David Vlijmincx

BIRMINGHAM—MUMBAI

Cloud-Native Development and Migration to Jakarta EE

Group Product Manager: Gebin George
Publishing Product Manager: Kunal Sawant
Senior Editor: Nithya Sadanandan
Technical Editor: Jubit Pincy
Copy Editor: Safis Editing
Project Coordinator: Deeksha Thakkar
Proofreader: Safis Editing
Indexer: Hemangini Bari
Production Designer: Ponraj Dhandapani
Marketing Coordinator: Sonia Chauhan
Business Development Executive: Samriddhi Murarka

First published: November 2023

Production reference: 3231023

Published by Packt Publishing Ltd.
Grosvenor House
11 St Paul's Square
Birmingham
B3 1R.

ISBN 978-1-83763-962-5

www.packtpub.com

For my loved ones, whose sacrifices made it possible for me to work on this book.

– Ron Veen

For Mariska and my parents, Bernadette and Frits.

– David Vlijmincx

Contributors

About the authors

Ron Veen is a highly experienced software engineer, navigating the spectrum from Midrange Systems to Micro Services. Driven by his passion for software engineering and software architecture, he has amassed more than 15 years of experience working on the JVM and the Java ecosystem. Ron has seen all the frameworks and libraries from Apache to ZK and has worked with many versions of Java EE and later, Jakarta EE. An avid fan of alternative JVM languages like Groovy, Scala, Clojure, and his personal favorite Kotlin, Ron is also an Oracle Certified Java Programmer (OCP) and Sun Certified Business Component Developer (SCBCD/OCPBCD). Ron is also a regular speaker at international conferences.

David Vlijmincx is a software developer with 8 years of experience in the field. He has a strong background in software development, with a focus on building scalable, high-quality applications using the Java programming language. David's expertise spans through a variety of projects, ranging from small, standalone applications to large, complex systems, which needed to be migrated to newer versions of the EE specification or the cloud. David is an Oracle Certified Java Programmer (OCP) and is an avid blogger and speaker at industry conferences.

About the reviewer

Edwin Derks, a distinguished Java Champion hailing from The Netherlands, excels in unraveling intricate and strategic IT challenges as a dedicated Consultant. He is passionate about gathering and sharing knowledge on various facets of the Java ecosystem, composable architectures, and cloud-driven development . He actively contributes to MicroProfile and Jakarta EE and often speaks at conferences, passionately sharing his knowledge and experience.

In his spare time, he is a loving husband and a father of three. He can often be found in the gym or having a good time at dance parties or heavy metal concerts.

Table of Contents

Part 2: Modern Jakarta EE

3

Moving from Java EE to Jakarta EE   33

4

Modernizing Your Application with the Latest Features   51

8

What Is Cloud Native? 119

9

Deploying Jakarta EE Applications in the Cloud 133

10

Introducing MicroProfile   149

Appendix A

Java EE to Jakarta EE names   165

Appendix B

As a Service   167

Index   171

Other Books You May Enjoy   178

Preface

Welcome to our comprehensive guide on *Cloud-Native Development and Migration to Jakarta EE*! In the pages of this book, you are about to embark on a transformative journey through the evolution of Jakarta EE, exploring its rich history and evolution.

Our aim is to unlock the complex world of Jakarta EE, guiding you through the migration and modernization of your existing applications. As you turn the pages, you will discover how to make your code compatible with the latest Jakarta EE version and leverage its modern features effectively.

The adventure doesn't stop there. We'll dive into the realm of cloud-native development as we demystify containers and introduce the Eclipse MicroProfile, a powerful tool in your toolkit. Together, we will transition your applications from local hardware to the limitless possibilities of the cloud. With our expert guidance, you will learn to deploy your Jakarta EE applications on Microsoft Azure, gaining hands-on experience in managing cloud resources.

But that's not all; the final leg of your journey explores the world of serverless architecture. Here, you will learn to design and run services that are truly serverless, harnessing the potential of the event-driven paradigm for scalability and cost-efficiency.

By the end of this book, you will not only be a Jakarta EE expert, but also a proficient cloud-native developer. So, join us on this exciting journey of transformation and innovation as you pave the way for the future of Jakarta EE and cloud-native development.

Who this book is for

This book is tailored for developers seeking valuable insights into how to migrate their applications from Java EE to Jakarta EE and seamlessly integrate them into a cloud environment. Within these pages, developers will find guidance on every step required to transition their applications from Java EE to the latest Jakarta EE version.

This book equips developers with the knowledge to modernize their applications with the latest features and to get it up and running in a cloud environment.

What this book covers

Chapter 1, *The History of Enterprise Java*, introduces you to the history of Java EE and Jakarta EE.

Chapter 2, *Introducing the Cargo Tracker Application*, starts with an overview of the Cargo tracker application's functionality. The second half takes a look at the Java EE features that are used in the project.

Chapter 3, *Moving from Java EE to Jakarta EE*, describes how to approach the migration from Java EE to Jakarta EE.

Chapter 4, *Modernizing Your Application with the Latest Features*, provides an overview of the significant changes made to Jakarta EE 10. The chapter will also show you how to implement cloud-native features like resilience and monitoring. Lastly, we will show you how to visualize the metrics coming from your application.

Chapter 5, *Making Your Application Testable*, provides an overview of why testing is important when migrating a software project and how to measure it. You will learn how to write unit tests and integration tests for modern applications to ensure the application keeps working as expected.

Chapter 6, *Introduction to Containers and Docker*, provides an overview of what containers are and why they are an important tool. You will learn what Docker is, how to install it, and how to create a Docker container based on the Cargo tracker application.

Chapter 7, *Meet Kubernetes*, introduces you to Kubernetes, the *de facto* standard for running containers.

Chapter 8, *What is Cloud Native?*, describes the principles of cloud-native computing.

Chapter 9, *Deploying Jakarta EE Applications in the Cloud*, provides an overview of deploying an application to the Azure cloud. You will learn how to create a container registry and how to create an instance from a container in the registry. This chapter also covers how you can see the metrics of the deployed instance.

Chapter 10, *Introducing MicroProfile*, introduces the most important specifications of the MicroProfile specification.

Appendix A, *Java EE to Jakarta EE names*, is a list of Java EE to Jakarta EE specifications.

Appendix B, *As a Service*, explains the different concepts of using the Internet for computing.

To get the most out of this book

For optimal learning, it is essential to have prior experience in developing Java applications using an enterprise framework like Java EE, Jakarta EE, or Spring.

Software/hardware covered in the book	Operating system requirements
Azure Cloud	Windows, macOS, or Linux
Java 17	
Java EE 7	
Jakarta EE 10	

If you are using the digital version of this book, we advise you to type the code yourself or access the code from the book's GitHub repository (a link is available in the next section). Doing so will help you avoid any potential errors related to the copying and pasting of code.

Download the example code files

You can download the example code files for this book from GitHub at `https://github.com/ PacktPublishing/Cloud-Native-Development-and-Migration-to-Jakarta-EE`. If there's an update to the code, it will be updated in the GitHub repository.

We also have other code bundles from our rich catalog of books and videos available at `https:// github.com/PacktPublishing/`. Check them out!

Conventions used

There are a number of text conventions used throughout this book.

`Code in text`: Indicates code words in text, database table names, folder names, filenames, file extensions, pathnames, dummy URLs, user input, and Twitter handles. Here is an example: "The `param-value` tells PrimeFaces that we want to use the `omega` theme for the project."

A block of code is set as follows:

```
<context-param>
    <param-name>primefaces.THEME</param-name>
    <param-value>saga</param-value>
</context-param>
```

When we wish to draw your attention to a particular part of a code block, the relevant lines or items are set in bold:

```
mvn compile
```

Any command-line input or output is written as follows:

Bold: Indicates a new term, an important word, or words that you see onscreen. For instance, words in menus or dialog boxes appear in **bold**. Here is an example: "If a quick fix can be applied, you can do so by right-clicking the incident and choosing **Apply All Quickfixes**."

> **Tips or important notes**
> Appear like this.

Get in touch

Feedback from our readers is always welcome.

General feedback: If you have questions about any aspect of this book, email us at `customercare@packtpub.com` and mention the book title in the subject of your message.

Errata: Although we have taken every care to ensure the accuracy of our content, mistakes do happen. If you have found a mistake in this book, we would be grateful if you would report this to us. Please visit `www.packtpub.com/support/errata` and fill in the form.

Piracy: If you come across any illegal copies of our works in any form on the internet, we would be grateful if you would provide us with the location address or website name. Please contact us at `copyright@packt.com` with a link to the material.

If you are interested in becoming an author: If there is a topic that you have expertise in and you are interested in either writing or contributing to a book, please visit `authors.packtpub.com`.

Share Your Thoughts

Once you've read *Cloud-Native Development and Migration to Jakarta EE*, we'd love to hear your thoughts! Scan the QR code below to go straight to the Amazon review page for this book and share your feedback.

`https://packt.link/r/1837639620`

Your review is important to us and the tech community and will help us make sure we're delivering excellent quality content.

Download a free PDF copy of this book

Thanks for purchasing this book!

Do you like to read on the go but are unable to carry your print books everywhere?

Is your eBook purchase not compatible with the device of your choice?

Don't worry, now with every Packt book you get a DRM-free PDF version of that book at no cost.

Read anywhere, any place, on any device. Search, copy, and paste code from your favorite technical books directly into your application.

The perks don't stop there, you can get exclusive access to discounts, newsletters, and great free content in your inbox daily

Follow these simple steps to get the benefits:

1. Scan the QR code or visit the link below

https://packt.link/free-ebook/9781837639625

2. Submit your proof of purchase

3. That's it! We'll send your free PDF and other benefits to your email directly

Part 1:
History of Java EE
and Jakarta EE

In this part, you will get an overview of the history of enterprise Java and the application we will be migrating throughout this book. The historical context will shed light on the transformation from Java EE and underscore the necessity of migrating to Jakarta EE 10. This will also include the changes that Jakarta EE made to make developing applications easier. The introduction of the Cargo tracker will help you familiarize yourself with the application, so you know what we are migrating and the challenges we'll encounter.

This part has the following chapters:

- *Chapter 1, The History of Enterprise Java*
- *Chapter 2, Introducing the Cargo Tracker Application*

1

The History of Enterprise Java

In this chapter, we will look at the history of Java EE and Jakarta EE. Since its inception, Java enterprise technology has had several names – starting as J2EE, then being rebranded as JEE, followed by Java EE, and finally, Jakarta EE.

In this chapter, we will cover the following topics:

- What is Java EE, and why was it created?
- Web servers versus application servers
- Java EE 5, the first user-friendly version
- The history of key features added in Java EE since version 5

By the end of this chapter, you will have a better understanding of Java EE and Jakarta EE in a historical sense, and you will know some of the key features added to Java EE. Changes to Jakarta EE will be discussed in subsequent chapters.

What is Java EE, and why was it created?

The Java language was introduced to the world in 1996. It consisted of a compiler and a Java virtual machine. Both components are platform-dependent, meaning that you have different versions for Windows, Linux, macOS, and so on. This is called **Java Standard Edition (Java SE)**.

The Java language is unique in that it does not compile to native machine code but, instead, to something called **bytecode**. This bytecode is platform-independent, meaning it can be transferred to any of the aforementioned platforms.

To execute the bytecode, you would need a **Java Virtual Machine (JVM)**. The JVM translates the intermediate bytecode to machine code, specific to the platform it is executed on.

This principle of compiling to bytecode and being able to execute it on any platform was dubbed **Write Once, Run Anywhere (WORA)**. This has proven to be the distinctive feature that has led to the success of Java in business environments.

Initially, Java was meant to run in browsers, inside so-called applets. These applets added a lot of functionality to the early browsers such as Microsoft's Internet Explorer and Netscape's Navigator.

Free versions of Java were supplied to several popular platforms, which aided in the rapid success of the language.

The JVM specification could be licensed by third parties, allowing them to build their own implementations of the compiler and the JVM. Several companies have done so, which means that there are now several vendors that offer their own implementation. The most common are (in alphabetical order) as follows:

- Alibabi Dragonwell
- Amazon Coretto
- Azul Zulu
- Bellsoft Liberica
- Eclipse Adoptium Temurin
- J9
- Oracle Oracle JDK and OpenJDK
- Redhat OpenJDK
- SAP SapMachine

But soon, Java moved out of the realm of browsers into the business world. It became obvious that developing business applications required additional functionality that was not part of the language.

Instead of adding this functionality to the language itself, it was decided that it would better be provided by a separate set of APIs. To avoid confusion and distinguish between Java SE and these new APIs, they were called **Java Enterprise Edition (Java EE)**.

Java EE added features such as transactions, security, scalability, management of components, and concurrency. It allowed you to create dynamic web applications and provided a robust platform for distributed transactions.

Web servers versus application servers

The terms **web servers** and **application servers** are often confused by people new to Java EE and used interchangeably, although this is not correct. In this section, we will highlight the differences between the two, as we believe that it is important to know the differences between them, as both are key components of Java EE, but each plays its own role.

Starting to understand the difference between them is best done by highlighting their goals.

Web servers

Web servers implement the Servlet API, which is a set of classes and interfaces defined in the specification that allow you to create dynamic web applications. Applications based on the Servlet API, called Servlets, run inside a web server and serve, possibly dynamic, content to their users.

There are a number of technologies developed over the years that support the Servlet API. Specifications such as **Java Server Pages (JSP)**, **Java Standard Tag Libraries (JSTL)**, **Java Server Faces (JSF)**, and Bean Validations are the most notable. Later, **Java API for XML Web Service (JAX-WS)** and **Java API for Restful Web services (JAX-RS)** were added.

There are many popular, standalone implementations of the Servlet API, such as the following:

- Tomcat
- Jetty
- NGINX

All these provide a Servlet container in which servlets can run.

It is good to understand that you can run multiple servlets inside one servlet container. In the early days, this was a common practice, as it allowed you to run more than one application on the same piece of hardware.

For good measure, it should be noted that a framework such as Spring Boot still uses the Servlet API. This means that at the core level, some implementation of the Servlet API is still running. In the case of Spring Boot, however, which servlet container implementation is being used is pluggable, meaning you choose it yourself.

Application servers

Conversely, application servers do have the requirement of supplying an implementation that supports the Servlet API, but they offer far more than that. Application servers offer a richer environment, more targeted at executing business logic. They offer **Enterprise Java Beans (EJBs)**. EJBs come in three major flavors:

- **Session Beans (SBs)**
- **Entity Beans (EBs)**
- **Message-Driven Beans (MDBs)**

Session beans can be further divided into **Stateful Session Beans (SFSBs)** and **Stateless Session Beans (SLSBs)**. Session beans contain business logic.

Entity beans, which handle database operations, came as **Container Managed Persistence (CMP)** and **Bean Managed Persistence (BMP)** entity beans. In the former, the application server was responsible for handling the persistence and retrieval of the data, while in the latter, an application developer had to write the queries to select and update the database themselves.

We write this in the past tense, as entity beans were dropped altogether in version 3 of the EJB specification, delivered in Java EE 5, in favor of the **Java Persistence API (JPA)**.

Furthermore, application servers provide APIs for declarative and programmatic transaction management. As with entity beans, the difference is that in the former, the container will start, commit, or roll back transactions automatically, while in the latter, this has to be done in code.

The **Java Messaging Service (JMS)** is another feature that is required for application servers. JMS allows you to asynchronously exchange messages between different applications or application components.

JMS offers one-to-one connections between two components via queues while offering a one-to-many message exchange via topics.

Furthermore, application servers allow the registration and discovery of components via the **Java Naming and Directory Interface (JNDI)**. As an example, an EJB to send emails can be instantiated and successively registered in the JNDI registry. Another EJB, which requires the functionality of sending an email, is then able to look up this email service by its name in the registry and use it.

In addition to this, functionality such as declarative security, concurrency, and interceptors are provided by application servers.

Some very popular application servers are as follows:

- IBM Websphere
- JBoss Application
- Oracle Glassfish
- Oracle Weblogic
- Payara Server Enterprise

Application servers had a tendency to be heavy, and startup times were awful. Taking 10–15 minutes to start up and bringing the deployed applications to an initialized state was quite common in the early days. However, nowadays, it is very common that they start within a few seconds.

Profiles to the rescue

In the early years of Java EE, there was one simple rule if you wanted to be a Java EE compatible server – you had to implement all the specifications. However, it soon became clear that not every application required a full-blown application server. Often, a web server was more than enough.

To make this distinction clearer, profiles were introduced. The first one was Web Profile, which made its first appearance in Java EE 6. It was made up of the Servlet, JSF, JSP, EJB, CDI, JTA, JPA, and Bean Validation specifications.

The full set of all specifications became known as the Full Platform Profile.

In Jakarta EE 10, the Core Profile was introduced. This contains an even smaller subset of specifications and targets microservices, edge-computing, and ahead-of-time compilation. In *Chapter 2*, we will dive deeper into these subjects.

The following diagram depicts the different profiles and the specifications they are required to implement. The image was taken from the Jakarta EE website (`https://jakarta.ee/release/10/`).

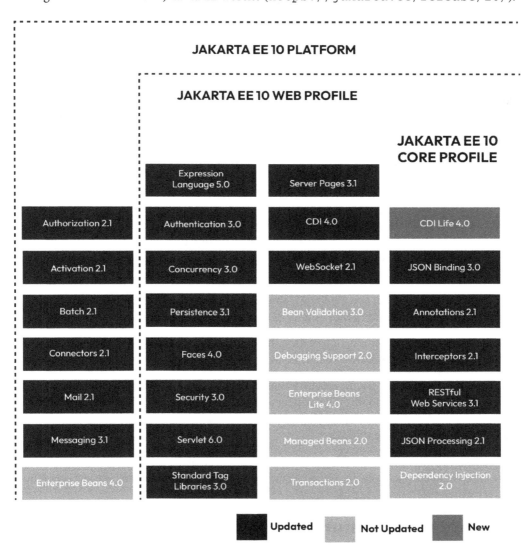

Figure 1.1 – The different Jakarta EE profiles and their specifications

Java EE 5, the first user-friendly version

This thing that hampered Java EE most of all was the sheer amount of configuration that you had to provide. All of these configurations had to be done in so-called XML deployment configuration files. We refer you to the documentation at `https://docs.oracle.com/cd/E13211_01/wle/dd/ddref.htm`, should you be interested in the content of the files.

For a container-managed entity bean, for instance, you had to specify each of the methods that were exported, its type parameters, and the return value.

It was not uncommon to have these configuration files being more than 300–400 lines of XML. This was called configuration hell, and this is where Java EE (back then still called J2EE) got its reputation in the developer community for being bloated.

Developers got so frustrated with this type of configuration that alternatives arose. The rise of the now very famous Spring Framework can be attributed to exactly these feelings. The Spring Framework itself required some XML configuration, but it wired up a lot of parts automatically for developers. Back then, what the Spring Framework did mostly, next to adding dependency injection, was wiring up the different components.

In 2005, version 5 of Java EE was released. This was the first time that J2EE was rebranded Java EE, but more importantly, it introduced annotations for the first time. Annotations allowed you to specify certain configuration options already in the code, thus providing a reasonable default setting. Now, it only was required to specify the situations where the configuration should divert from these default values. This is called convention over configuration, and it immensely reduces the amount of configuration required.

Another improvement was that you could now simply annotate a bean with, for instance, `@Local`, to define it as a local EJB. Again, dozens of lines of configuration were saved.

This was actually part of the introduction of the EJB3 specification. It was revolutionary in that sense that it deprecated the traditional entity beans in favor of the **Java Persistence API(JPA)**.

JPA was heavily influenced by frameworks such as Hibernate, which provided an object-relational persistence approach. This meant that the mapping between database fields and Java fields was done by the framework now; no longer was application code required to achieve this mapping. This is known as **Object-Relational Mapping (ORM)**.

With Java EE version 5, a very competitive and, maybe for the first time, very developer-friendly version of the specification became available. Suddenly, developing Java EE applications was not something just for very experienced developers anymore.

The history of key features added in Java EE since version 5

Let us now have a quick look at what changes have been introduced in Java EE after version 5.

Java EE 6

The most famous change that was introduced in Java EE version 6 is undoubtedly the support for RESTful API web services. REST has become the more popular form of web service, compared to SOAP web services, due to its flexible nature.

Additionally, version 6 saw the introduction of the **Context and Dependency Injection (CDI)** API. That allowed for, among other things, the use of dependency injection in Java EE applications.

Java EE 7

Java EE version 7 introduced the notion of batch applications. These are a number of tasks that are executed without user intervention.

It also introduced some additional concurrency utilities, such as the managed executor service, a scheduled variant, and a managed thread factory.

Furthermore, the first version of the WebSocket API was introduced. WebSockets allow full duplex communication between two peers.

Finally, the introduction of the JSON-P specification should not go unmentioned. It allows Java objects to be serialized to the JSON format, and vice versa. This has, with the rise of the RESTful API web services, become a pivotal specification of the Java EE platform.

Java EE 8

Java EE 8 was the final version of Java EE released by Oracle. The was a considerable amount of time between the release of Java EE version 7 and version 8 (4 years, 3 months, and 3 days to be exact). It was starting to become clear that Java EE was in demise at Oracle.

Nevertheless, this final version introduced some good functionality. Most of all, there was JAXB, the Java API for XML binding. Furthermore, annotation-based security was introduced with the Java Security EE API.

Summary

This chapter has given a short introduction to the history of Java EE up to version 8. After this version, Java EE was handed over to the Eclipse Foundation and was rebranded as Jakarta EE.

With this history in mind, you can now start your Jakarta EE journey. In the next chapter, we will introduce our example application to you, while in the following chapters, we will start migrating to a newer version of Jakarta EE.

2

Introducing the Cargo Tracker Application

In this chapter, we will introduce the Cargo Tracker application, which was built using Java EE 7. We will use the Cargo Tracker application throughout this book. This is the application we will migrate from Java EE 7 to Jakarta EE 10. Before we start migrating the application, it is good to understand the Cargo Tracker application. This chapter will provide an overview of the Cargo Tracker application and its features, as well as its current architecture and design.

Additionally, we will go through the various components of the Cargo Tracker application and how they interact with each other. We will cover topics such as the use of REST, WebSockets, and **JavaServer Faces** (**JSF**) for presentation, **Enterprise Java Beans** (**EJB**) for business logic, and **Java Persistence** (**JPA**) for data persistence. We will also highlight the use of **Contexts and Dependency Injection** (**CDI**) for dependency management between components.

In this chapter, we will cover the following topics:

- Installing and running the Cargo Tracker application
- What can the Cargo Tracker application do?
- Java EE features used in the Cargo Tracker application

By the end of this chapter, you will have a solid understanding of the Cargo Tracker application and its underlying technology stack. This will serve as a foundation for the rest of this book, where we will delve deeper into the specifics of migrating the Cargo Tracker application to Jakarta EE 10.

Technical requirements

To get started with the Cargo Tracker application, you will need the following tools. They will allow you to download and create a version of the Cargo Tracker application that we can run locally:

- An editor of your choice – for example, JetBrains IntelliJ, Eclipse IDE, or Microsoft Visual Code
- Git
- JDK 8
- Maven 3

You must also have a JAVA_HOME environment variable that points to the JDK 8 home directory.

What is the Cargo Tracker application?

The Cargo Tracker application is a Java EE application that was developed to show some of the capabilities of the Java EE platform. It was built with best practices such as domain-driven design. The application is meant to be easy to understand, while still highlighting the strength of many Java EE technologies. The Cargo Tracker application is used to track and route cargo that's been booked in the application. It contains functionality to book cargo at a certain port and choose a route for the cargo, and an event viewer to publish events that the system reacts to.

The Cargo Tracker application has multiple versions/branches that use a different version of Java or Jakarta EE. For this book, we are interested in the version of the Cargo Tracker application that uses Java EE 7.

Java EE 7 can be used with both Java 7 and Java 8. However, the developers of the Cargo Tracker application used some language features that are only available in Java 8. Because of this, we need to use Java 8. Java 8 is a large and influential version of Java that delivers things such as Streams, lambdas, and a new date API.

Why we chose the Cargo Tracker application

It is hard to find open source projects that focus on Java EE technology. The reason for this is simple: these types of applications are used in a business environment and deal with fine-grained business logic. Very few people have the combined knowledge of technology and business rules, let alone the time to start such a project.

Naturally, we could not use the sources from closed source projects as we would not be able to share the sources with you.

Luckily, the Cargo Tracker application meets all the demands we have for a demo application. It is open source, uses a fair amount of Java EE technology, and is still simple enough to understand even for those not familiar with the shipping business.

Installing and running the Cargo Tracker application

Before we can install and run the Cargo Tracker application, we need to get the source code from the official repository on GitHub. The first step is to clone the project to a local directory. To do so, open a Terminal or command prompt and run the following command:

```
git clone https://github.com/eclipse-ee4j/cargotracker.git
```

This command will create a directory called `cargotracker` and copy the source code from GitHub into the directory. The next step is to go into the directory so that we can change the branch of the project. For this, use the following command:

```
cd .\cargotracker\
```

Now that we are in the correct directory, we can change the branch using this command:

```
git checkout javaee7
```

After you run this command, you will have a version of the Cargo Tracker application that uses Java EE 7. This will be the starting point of the source code for migrating to Jakarta EE 10.

With the source code ready, we can start running the project for the first time. Using a new or existing Terminal or command prompt, navigate to the `cargotracker` directory. Use the following command to run the project using Maven Cargo:

```
mvn package cargo:run
```

Starting the project for the first time may take a while because Maven must download dependencies for the Cargo Tracker application. Once the download has finished, it will continue building the project. Once you see the following text in the console, you will know that the project has finished building and is ready to use:

```
[INFO] [talledLocalContainer] Command deploy executed successfully.
[INFO] [talledLocalContainer] GlassFish 4.1.2.181 started on port
[8080]
[INFO] Press Ctrl-C to stop the container…
```

When you see this in the console, use your favorite browser and navigate to http://localhost:8080/cargo-tracker/. This is the home page of the Cargo Tracker application. If your browser looks as follows, you'll know that the Cargo Tracker application has been successfully deployed:

Figure 2.1 – Cargo Tracker start screen

With this, we have successfully installed and run our Cargo Tracker application. Using the three links on the screen, you can navigate to various parts of the Cargo Tracker application. Let's learn how to do that.

Features of the Cargo Tracker application

Before we can start migrating the Cargo Tracker application, it is important to have a good understanding of the application. This understanding will serve as the foundation for the entire migration process and increase the project's success. By having a clear understanding of the application, you will be able to identify classes, modules, or features, as well as potential challenges that need to be addressed. This will help us make informed decisions about the migration process, reduce risks, and ensure a smooth migration project. In this section, we'll delve deeper into the various features of the Cargo Tracker application.

Public Tracking Interface

This page is intended for users who are tracking their cargo. They can use this page to look up the status of their cargo as it goes through the system. When you click on the **Public Tracking Interface** link, you'll see the following screen:

Figure 2.2 – Tracking interface

If, for example, you enter a tracking ID of ABC123 in the **Enter your tracking ID** field and press the **Track!** button, you will see the status of the cargo on the screen. This will look as follows:

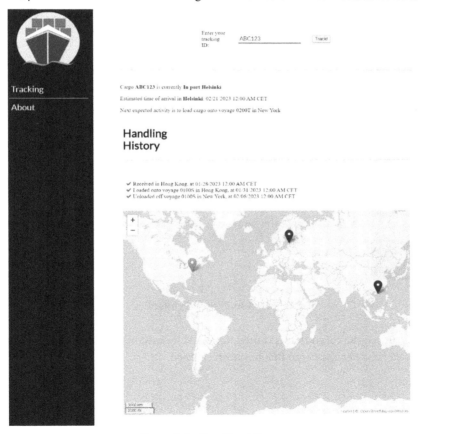

Figure 2.3 – Handling History

The screen shows you the following:

- Where the cargo with an ID of ABC123 currently is
- The estimated time of arrival at the destination, Helsinki
- What is the next expected activity
- The handling history
- A map of the world with a marker of where the handling activity has happened

Administration Interface

This interface is for users who manage the different cargo, voyagers, and their routes. It shows you all the information about the cargo that is in the system:

Routed Cargo

Tracking ID	Origin	Destination	Last Known Location	Status	Deadline
ABC123	Hong Kong	Helsinki	New York	IN_PORT	02/22/2023
	CNHKG	FIHEL	USNYC		
JKL567	Hangzhou	Stockholm	New York	ONBOARD_CARRIER	02/25/2023
	CNHGH	SESTO	USNYC		

Not Routed Cargo

Tracking ID	Origin	Destination	Deadline
DEF789	Hong Kong	Melbourne	04/07/2023
	CNHKG	AUMEL	

Claimed Cargo

Tracking ID	Origin	Destination	Deadline
MNO456	New York	Dallas	01/14/2023
	USNYC	USDAL	

Figure 2.4 – Administration Interface

At the top, you can see the cargo that is routed, followed by cargo that has not been routed. At the bottom of the page, you can see cargo that has been claimed.

Details about cargo

When you click on the tracking ID of a routed cargo, you get a new screen that shows you more cargo information. If we click on tracking ID ABC123, we will see the following screen:

Routing Details for Cargo ABC123

Origin: Hong Kong CNHKG

Destination: Helsinki FIHEL

Arrival deadline: 02/22/2023

Itinerary

Voyage	Load	Date	Unload	Date
0100S	Hong Kong CNHKG	01/31/2023	New York USNYC	02/06/2023
0200T	New York USNYC	02/09/2023	Dallas USDAL	02/13/2023
0300A	Dallas USDAL	02/15/2023	Helsinki FIHEL	02/21/2023

Figure 2.5 – Routing details

This page shows you more information about the cargo, such as its origin port, destination, and deadline for arrival. At the bottom, you will see the itinerary that belongs to this cargo.

Routing cargo

To route cargo, you first must select a piece of cargo from the **Not Routed Cargo** section in the administration interface. To start routing a piece of cargo, click on any tracking ID that hasn't been routed yet.

When you click on any of the IDs, you will see the following screen, which shows a few routes that are possible options for the selected cargo:

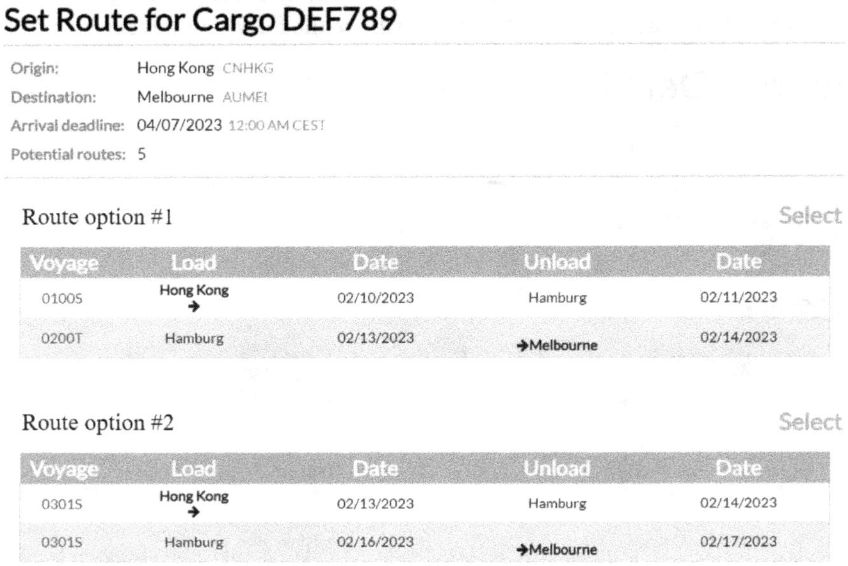

Set Route for Cargo DEF789

Origin:	Hong Kong CNHKG
Destination:	Melbourne AUMEL
Arrival deadline:	04/07/2023 12:00 AM CEST
Potential routes:	5

Route option #1   Select

Voyage	Load	Date	Unload	Date
0100S	Hong Kong ➔	02/10/2023	Hamburg	02/11/2023
0200T	Hamburg	02/13/2023	➔Melbourne	02/14/2023

Route option #2   Select

Voyage	Load	Date	Unload	Date
0301S	Hong Kong ➔	02/13/2023	Hamburg	02/14/2023
0301S	Hamburg	02/16/2023	➔Melbourne	02/17/2023

Figure 2.6 – Routing cargo interface

When you click on any of the route options, that route will be selected for the cargo. With a route selected, the status of the cargo will change from `not routed` to `routed`.

When we go back to the overview in the administrative interface, we'll see that the cargo is no longer listed in the **Not Routed Cargo** section but in the **Routed Cargo** section:

Routed Cargo

Tracking ID	Origin	Destination	Last Known Location	Status	Deadline
ABC123 ⓘ	Hong Kong CNHKG	Helsinki FIHEL	New York USNYC	IN_PORT	02/22/2023
JKL567 ⓘ	Hangzhou CNHGH	Stockholm SESTO	New York USNYC	ONBOARD_CARRIER	02/25/2023
DEF789 ⓘ	Hong Kong CNHKG	Melbourne AUMEL	Unknown location	NOT_RECEIVED	04/07/2023

Figure 2.7 – Cargo with a route

Booking cargo

When you click on **Book** on the left-hand side of the screen, you will be taken to the interface, which guides you through the process of booking a piece of cargo:

Figure 2.8 – Booking cargo interface

The first step in this process is to select a port from which the new cargo will be sent. In this example, I will choose **Chicago**. When you press Next, you will be asked to select a destination for the **cargo**:

Figure 2.9 – Selecting the cargo's destination

I've chosen **Tokyo** and pressed **Next**. The next question will be regarding the arrival deadline for the cargo, which must be a future date:

3. Set the arrival deadline for this new Chicago-Tokyo cargo

◄		April 2023				►
S	M	T	W	T	F	S
						1
2	3	4	5	6	7	8
9	10	11	12	13	14	15
16	17	18	19	20	21	22
23	24	25	26	27	28	29
30						

Journey duration is 79 days.

Back   Cancel   Book Cargo

Figure 2.10 – Booking the cargo's arrival date

Select any date for the cargo and click on **Book Cargo** to book the cargo into the system. When you click this button, you will be brought back to the administration interface, but the cargo we just booked will be shown under the **Not Routed Cargo** section:

Not Routed Cargo

Tracking ID	Origin	Destination	Deadline
DEF789 ⊙	Hong Kong CNHKG	Melbourne AUMEL ☑	04/07/2023 ☑
5B32EFBD ⊙	Chicago USCHI	Tokyo JNTKO ☑	04/27/2023 ☑

Figure 2.11 – Cargo without a route

Mobile Event Logger

Mobile Event Logger is an interface that's used to send events to the Cargo Tracker application. You can use the interface to manipulate the data inside the system. It enables you to move the cargo throughout the system.

To show you what this interface does, we will show you how to send an event for the cargo with an ID of DEF789 to the backend of the Cargo Tracker application. Here, we will send an event for the cargo with an ID of DEF789 to tell the system that it has arrived in Dallas.

When you click on the mobile event viewer, you will see the following screen, which guides us through the event creation process:

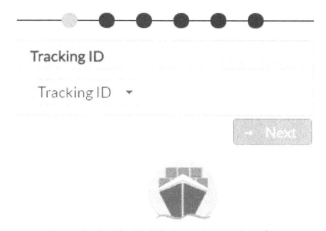

Figure 2.12 – The Mobile Event Logger interface

To create the event that we want, follow these steps:

1. Select the tracking ID of DEF789 from the drop-down list.

2. Click the **Next** button.

3. Select the location of where the cargo had arrived – for example, Dallas.

4. Click the **Next** button.

5. Select the **UNLOAD** event type.

6. Select the voyage the cargo is currently on. In our case, this is **0301S**.

7. Click the **Next** button.

8. Select the date on which the event occurred. In our case, I selected **16-02-2023**.

9. Click the **Next** button.

After following these steps, you will be shown a confirmation screen that shows all the information you filled in during the previous steps. Check that they are correct; if they are, you can click the **Submit** button, which will send the event to the Cargo Tracker application.

When we look at the administrative interface, we will see that the cargo's status is now **IN_PORT** and that the last known location is Dallas for the cargo with an ID of DEF789.

Java EE features used in the Cargo Tracker application

Now that you have an idea of how the Cargo Tracker application works, it is time to look at the technologies involved in making it work. Java EE consists of multiple projects and technologies where each of the projects can leverage the functionalities of the other.

The Cargo Tracker application uses a lot of Java EE functionality. In the next few sections, we will walk through those that are mostly used. We will briefly describe what the functionality is and how it is used with the Cargo Tracker application.

Will be using the Java EE naming of these technologies. Jakarta EE has different names for these technologies. We will discuss the following Java EE 7 technologies:

- Enterprise Java Beans
- Java Persistence
- Java Messaging System
- Context and Dependency Injection
- Java Server Faces
- JAX-RS
- JSON-B)
- Java Batch

Note that during the switch from Java EE to Jakarta EE, the names of many technologies had to be changed due to legal requirements. In *Appendix A*, you can find a list that compares the technologies by the original Java EE name and its new Jakarta EE name.

Enterprise Java Beans

Enterprise Beans have been around since day one. In the "old" days of J2EE, there were several different types of enterprise beans: **Session Beans (SB)**, **Entity Beans (EB)**, and **Message Driven Beans (MDB)**.

Session beans can be further subdivided into Stateful Session Beans, Stateless Session Beans, and Singleton Session Beans. While the former two have always been around, the latter was added in version 3.x of the specification.

Stateful Session Beans maintain a conversational state with a client. This means that the client has a one-to-one connection with a specific bean and that this bean only serves that client for the duration of the conversation. For example, we can have `ShoppingCartSession` that connects with a `Faces` shopping cart.

Stateless Session Beans have no knowledge of what clients they had a conversation with during their life cycle. The application server typically pools them. Once a request for Stateless Session Beans arrives at this application, a bean is selected from the pool and the requested method is invoked on it. Stateless Beans provide the container with a great level of flexibility as it can increase or decrease the pool size as it seems fit.

The final kind of session bean is the Singleton Session Bean. This one works just like a stateless session, but there is only ever one instance of this bean for the whole application. Singleton Session Beans are typically used for tasks such as upgrading the database or other batch-related tasks.

Moving on to the next kind of Enterprise Beans, we have the Entity Beans. These beans were introduced in version 1.0 of the specification and came in two flavors: **Bean Managed Persistence** (**BMP**) and **Container Managed Persistence** (**CMP**). The former left it to the application developer to invoke persistence operations and perform transaction management, while the latter left it up to the EJB container to invoke the appropriate data retrieval/store and transaction control operations. These types of beans became very unpopular since all the operations and parameters needed to be specified in a special deployment descriptor file (`ejb-jar.xml`), leading to XML files that more frequently than not contained several hundreds of XML statements. They became so unpopular that in version 3 of the Enterprise Beans specification, they were dropped altogether in favor of Java Persistence.

The final type of bean is the Message Driven Bean. This is a specialized form of bean that's registered as a consumer of JMS (or Messaging) messages placed on a queue or topic. Once a message arrives on the queue or topic, this beans' callback method will be invoked to execute some business logic.

Persistence (JPA)

As mentioned earlier, Java Persistence is the replacement for Entity Beans. JPA should be seen in the widest sense: creating, updating, retrieving, deleting, and querying. Objects that are to be persisted are annotated with the `@Entity` annotation. Moreover, relationships between entities can be modeled in code.

JPA was heavily influenced by the ideas and concepts of Hibernate, a popular object-relational mapper. It tried to offer a workaround for the fact that, in code, we work with objects that can embed other objects while once persisting or retrieving data, we work with flat tables.

JPA also offers possibilities for querying data via conventional SQL, an object-oriented query DSL, and object-based query definitions called the Criteria API.

Messaging (JMS)

JMS is the concept by which disjoint systems can integrate through the exchange of messages. Messaging is certainly not something that was invented by Java EE. Even before the rise of Java, there were many implementations of this so-called **message-oriented middleware** (**MoM**). Examples include IBM MQ and Tibco Messaging Service. More recently, Apache Kafka attracted enormous attention inside and outside of the Java community. JMS provided a specification for a standard way of working for messaging.

JMS supports two types of messaging: **point-to-point (PTP)** and **publish and subscribe (pub-sub)**. PTP works with queues, which is a place where the two clients involved in the messaging process can exchange messages between one another. So, this is typically a one-to-one connection. Pub-sub, on the other hand, works in such a way that one client will post messages on a topic and an unbound number of clients will show their interest in receiving these messages by subscribing to this topic.

One of the main advantages of asynchronous communication via messaging is that a system is not influenced heavily by the unavailability of the intended receiving system. To the sending system, the message still appears to be sent. It will sit idle in the queue until the receiving system comes online to retrieve it. Compare this to a situation in which a direct call is made into another system (for instance, via REST) and this system would not be available. This might lead to all kinds of problems due to the synchronous way of coupling the two systems. Now, increase the number of connected systems and you will start to see why messaging is such a brilliant solution.

Context and Dependency Injection

CDI is the Context and Dependency Injection API. It is obvious that over the years, Java EE was heavily pressured and influenced by the Spring framework. CDI is the best example of this as the Spring framework popularized **dependency injection (DI)**. DI is the concept that an object should not instantiate itself the objects it requires, but rather have these objects injected into it. DI encourages you to have an **inversion of control (IoC)** for dependency injection, and CDI builds upon that specification.

Next to injecting objects in a class at runtime, CDI also has the concept of producers. These are not the dependent objects themselves but objects that know how to get the dependent object.

CDI is not just about injecting dependent objects, though – it also provides an event mechanism. This allows one bean to fire an event while another bean has registered itself as being interested in these events. So, once the event is fired, a listener class can react to it. As an example, imagine a bean called `CustomerRegistrationBean` that will fire a `CustomerCreatedEvent` event. The `EmailBean` bean will listen for these events and upon receiving the `CustomerCreatedEvent` event, it will send out a welcome email to the new customer.

It is good to point out that CDI is not the only dependency injection mechanism available in Jakarta EE. Since version 3.0, EJB has 0 supported annotations for dependency injection:

- `@EJB`
- `@Resource`

`@EJB` allows you to inject other EJBs into an EJB, while `@Resource` allows you to inject program objects that provide connections to other systems, such as a SQL DataSource or a Jakarta Messaging MessageFactory.

Other APIs might supply injection annotations. An example of this is the @PersistenceUnit annotation from JPA, which will inject an EntityManagerFactory object.

Java Service Faces (JSF)

JSF is a server-side component-based user interface framework. It is one of the techniques available for rendering user interfaces in a browser. There have been many iterations for UI development in Java EE, starting with basic servlets, where the HTML was written to an output stream. Then, there was the addition of **Java Server Pages (JSP)**, which allow for a separation between business and presentation logic. Then, there came support for custom tag libraries and a standard tag library set, **Java Standard Tag Library (JSTL)**. Finally, there was JSF.

JSF follows the famous **model-view-control (MVC)** pattern. It is a collection of UI widgets and controls. As it is a specification, many competing implementations have arisen over time. Famous examples are IceFaces, OpenFaces, and MyFaces.

The process works as follows: you have a web page on which you add JSF custom tags, which represent UI elements. Each page has one or more so-called backing beans. Backing beans are managed by the container runtime and they serve to hold properties and methods for the UI elements. Furthermore, they can hold event listeners.

As a simple example, have a look at the following JSF, which has been taken from the Hello World example of the Jakarta EE tutorial:

```
<html lang="en"
    <h:body>
        <h:form>
            <h:graphicImage url="#{resource['images:duke.waving.gif']}"
             alt="Duke waving his hand"/>
            <h2>Hello, my name is Duke. What's yours?</h2>
            <h:inputText id="username"
                        title="My name is: "
                        value="#{hello.name}"
                        required="true"
                        requiredMessage="Error: A name is required."
                        maxlength="25" />
            <p></p>
            <h:commandButton id="submit" value="Submit"
             action="response">
            </h:commandButton>
            <h:commandButton id="reset" value="Reset" type="reset">
            </h:commandButton>
        </h:form>
        . . .
    </h:body>
</html>
```

Here, the `<h:inputText>` element defines a field for text entry, while `<h:commandButton>` defines a button on which to click. All these elements are prefixed with h, which is a shortcut for the JSF namespace.

Here is the code for the backing bean of the JSF page:

```
@Named
@RequestScoped
public class Hello {
    private String name;
    public Hello() {
    }
    public String getName() {
        return name;
    }
    public void setName(String user_name) {
        this.name = user_name;
    }
}
```

The `inputText` field is connected to the `name` property of the backing bean with the `value="#{hello.name}"` declaration, where `hello` is the name of the bean class, starting with lowercase, and `name` matches the `'name'` property in the backing bean.

The Cargo Tracker application uses JSF for all UI elements. If you want to browse the source code for the JSF pages, go to `src/main/webapp`.

JAX-RS

For a long time, SOAP was king in the land of web services. Java supported SOAP via JAX-WS, the Java API for XML web services. But at the beginning of the new century, a new type of web service made its entry. Roy Fielding authored a dissertation on this new concept and named it **REpresentational State Transfer**, or **REST** for short.

RESTful web services, those that follow the REST principles, are a way to expose resources on a machine in such a way that they can be accessed from other machines or services. Where SOAP web services impose strict rules upon the developers, RESTful web services can be developed in many programming languages. In contrast to SOAP, which only allows XML as its content, RESTful services support a variety of data formats. It is important to understand that REST uses the standard HTTP verbs (`GET`, `POST`, `PUT`, `PATCH`, `DELETE`, and `HEAD`) to perform its operations.

REST became extremely popular as it allowed an organization to share its data and information with the outside world in a remarkably simple, easy-to-understand way. In 2002 Jeff Bezos, the founder of Amazon, wrote a memo in which he mandated that "*all teams should expose their data and functions via service interfaces, that all teams must communicate with each other through these service interfaces, and finally that there no other form of inter-communication will be allowed.*" While Amazon was not the first large company to adapt REST, doing so in this rigorous way made way for its growth.

The following diagram shows the staggering growth of public APIs since 2005:

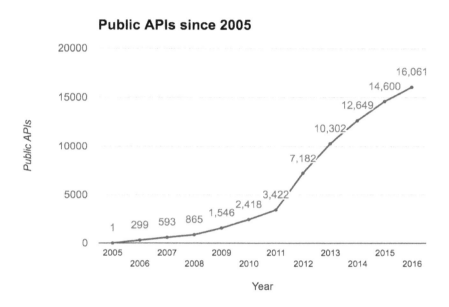

Figure 2.13 – The rise in the availability of public APIs

Since those beginning days, the number of public APIs based on REST has steadily grown, so much in fact that it is safe to say that REST is now the most common type of web service.

JSON binding

JSON binding is an API specification for the serialization of Java objects to JSON and vice versa. JSON is a simple format for representing data. It is often used instead of XML because it is less verbose. By default, it supports the default Java simple data types and their object counterparts. In addition to these, several date/time-related classes from the java.util package are supported and most classes from the java.time package. The (de-)serialization of many collection interfaces, such as List, Map, and Set, and their implementations in the java.util package is also supported out of the box.

Binding a JSON payload from a RESTful call to its object counterpart is mostly done automatically by the Java EE REST API runtime. Likewise, converting the resulting object of a RESTful call into JSON is also handled automatically by the Java EE REST API runtime.

Still, there might be situations where you would like to do these conversions yourself in code – for instance, to have more control over the conversion project by using any of the many conversion options.

By default, the mapping is done based on matching a JSON property name to a Java instance variable name. The JSON `firstname` property in the following JSON will be mapped on the Java `firstname` instance variable in the Java `Person` class.

The process of (de-)serialization can be influenced by adding annotations at the class level, instance variable level, or instance method level. The JSON `familyname` property will be mapped on the Java `name` instance variable as the `@JsonProperty("familyname")` annotation overrides the default mapping:

```
{
"familyname": "Mc Nealy",
"firstname": "Scott"
}
```

```
public class Person {
    @JsonProperty("familyname")
    private String name;
    private String firstname;
```

The Cargo Tracker application does not use annotation or automatic (de-)serialization. Instead, it uses programmatic conversion, as can be seen in the `CargoMonitoringService` class in the `org.eclipse.cargotracker.interfaces.booking.rest` package.

Transactions

One of the fundamental features of business data is integrity. Should this be lost, any decision-making on this data becomes walking on quicksand. Transactions help maintain data integrity.

It does this in two ways; firstly, by controlling concurrent access to the data and secondly, by restoring the data to its previous state in case of a system failure. The outcome of a transaction can only ever be one of two possibilities: either the operations performed concluded successfully and a commit is performed, or some kind of error occurred, and a rollback is performed. A commit will persist the outcome of the operation – for example, it will store the updated values in the database. A rollback, however, will restore the system to the state it was in before starting the transaction.

Java EE supports two types of transaction management: **Container Managed Transactions (CMTs)** and **Bean Managed Transactions (BMTs)**. If nothing is specified on an EJB, CMTs are the default mechanism.

With CMTs, the EJB container takes full control of starting, committing, and rolling back transactions. By default, the container will add transaction management to every public method in an EJB. If you would like to exclude certain public methods from running inside transactions, you can do so by specifying `TransactionAttribute` on the method.

In BMTs, the code in the EJB programmatically defines the boundaries of the transaction. This means that a transaction is started, committed, or rolled back in code. A transaction that's started in a method call to a stateless session bean must always be completed when that method completes.

The Cargo Tracker application uses CMTs with the `@Transactional` and `@TransactionAttribute` annotations to configure transaction management.

Batch

The Java EE platform contains functionality to run batch jobs. These are jobs that can run without any user interaction required. Examples of batch jobs are end-of-month processing in financials, generating reports, or periodically checking the filesystem for new files that need to be processed.

One thing each of these batch jobs has in common is that they consist of one or more steps that need to be executed. In Java EE, a batch job and its steps are described in an XML file. Each step is either a **Chunk** or a **Task**. Chunk steps can be executed in multiple threads simultaneously, while Tasks cannot.

Several steps grouped together are called a **flow**. Once grouped, they are executed as a unit. Several flows that can be executed in parallel are called **split**.

Summary

There is a lot of great technology inside the Cargo Tracker application. It is an application that was built to highlight that Java EE is a great framework for building applications. In this book, we are going to migrate the Cargo Tracker application to the even better Jakarta EE framework.

The application is made to book new cargo and keep track of the booked cargo. The tracker view shows you the status of the cargo. The administrative interface shows the status and lets you book and route cargo.

We also introduced some of the Java EE technologies used in the Cargo Tracker application and explained their usage.

Part 2:

Modern Jakarta EE

In this part, we will show you how to modernize the Cargo tracker application. Equipped with the necessary knowledge, you'll learn how to apply these techniques to other applications that require migration We cover the different tools you can use to migrate from Java EE to Jakarta EE and how these tools work. With an application that uses Jakarta EE 10, we'll show you how to modernize it and use best practices to make the application cloud-native while maintaining robust test coverage.

This part has the following chapters:

- *Chapter 3, Moving from Java EE to Jakarta EE*
- *Chapter 4, Modernizing Your Application with the Latest Features*
- *Chapter 5, Making Your Application Testable*

3

Moving from Java EE to Jakarta EE

In the previous chapter, you got to know the workings and technical details of the Cargo Tracker application. You should feel quite familiar now with the functionality of the application and have a basic understanding of the underlying technologies.

In this chapter, we're going to cover the following main topics:

- Migrating namespaces
- Migrating dependencies
- Upgrading your application server

Upgrading to **Jakarta EE9** is the first step to making the existing application work with the **Jakarta EE specifications**. We deliberately chose this method because we learned from experience that this is the easier approach. Once we are completely in the **Jakarta EE** ecosystem, we can start upgrading to new functionality delivered in **Jakarta EE 10**. This will be covered in the next chapter.

Technical requirements

You will need some tooling to migrate the namespaces. Some of these tools are operating system-dependent. You should choose the method that suits your specific situation best. There will be more than one option available for each of the major operating systems: **Linux**, **Windows**, and **macOS**.

Some of the solutions provided here will require the presence of additional software: some open source, and some that require a paid license.

You will also need an editor or **integrated development environment** (IDE) of some kind to change some source code. We will leave it up to you to select your tool of choice.

It's all about namespaces

When Oracle transferred Java EE to the Eclipse Foundation, no one could have foreseen what was to happen next. The Eclipse Foundation and its many volunteers started to work on updating the code and documentation to reflect the change from Oracle to the Eclipse Foundation. The negotiation took months in an attempt to agree upon the evolution of the javax package namespace in the Jakarta EE specifications. Unfortunately, due to insurmountable copyright issues, this undertaking failed. As a consequence, the javax namespace may only be used "as-is" with the Jakarta component specification, meaning that any specification that will evolve over time will need to change its namespace from the Java EE specification to a Jakarta EE specification. Also, the acronyms needed to be changed; for example, **Enterprise Java Beans (EJB)** became Jakarta Enterprise Beans.

Version 8 was the last version of the Java EE specification. Jakarta EE version 8 is completely the same but built from the source code at Eclipse.

Jakarta EE 9 is functionally equal to Jakarta EE 8, but the namespaces have now been renamed from javax to jakarta.

The following is an overview of all the changed namespaces with their original acronyms and their new namespace and acronyms.

Java EE namespace	Jakarta EE namespace
javax.activation	jakarta.activation
javax.annotation	jakarta.annotation
javax.batch	jakarta.batch
javax.cache	jakarta.cache
javax.decorator	jakarta.decorator
javax.ejb	jakarta.ejb
javax.el	jakarta.el
javax.enterprise	jakarta.enterprise
javax.inject	jakarta.inject
javax.interceptor	jakarta.interceptor
javax.jms	jakarta.jms
javax.json	jakarta.json
javax.jws	jakarta.jws
javax.management	jakarta.management
javax.persistence	jakarta.persistence
javax.resource	jakarta.resource

javax.security	jakarta.security
javax.servlet	jakarta.servlet
javax.transaction	jakarta.transaction
javax.validation	jakarta.validation
javax.websocket	jakarta.websocket
javax.ws	jakarta.ws
javax.xml	jakarta.xml

Table 3.1 – Namespace changes

Migrating strategies

Out of all of this, the most painful part from an application developer's point of view is that the namespaces have changed. This means that migrating to Jakarta involves refactoring all the Java EE import statements in your code base. To a lesser degree, changes need to be made to the POM files of your project as well.

In this section, we will look at three approaches to migrating your projects. We will do so using the following:

- An open source multiplatform editor
- The Sed command line tool
- A specialized plugin for your IDE

But before doing so, it is perhaps best to first create a new branch in Git that will contain our updated source code.

Enter the following command inside the cargotracker directory:

git checkout -b jakarta-ee9

Git will respond with the message Switched to a new branch 'jakarta-ee9.

If you would like to push this new local branch to your remote server immediately, you can do so by entering the following command:

git push -u origin jakarta-ee9:jakarta-ee9

You might prefer to make the necessary changes first before committing and pushing. In those circumstances, you skip pushing the new branch to the remote server right now.

Using an open source multiplatform editor

This conversion option will run on any of the major operating systems. We are using the open source editor Sublime Text, which can be downloaded from https://www.sublimetext.com/.

The editor has a **Find in Files** option, which recursively searches a directory tree for a certain text in a specified group of files.

Start the editor, select **Find in files...** from the **Find** drop-down menu, and either perform the following steps or enter the information shown in *Figure 3.1*:

1. In the **Find** text field enter javax.activation.
2. Press the button labeled ... located between Find and Replace.
3. Select **Add Folder**.
4. Choose your cargo tracker root directory from the selection dialog.
5. Press the button labeled ... again
6. Select **Add Include Filter**.
7. A text labeled *.txt will be inserted into the **Where** text field.
8. Change *.txt to *.java.
9. In the **Replace** text field, enter jakarta.activation.

Figure 3.1 – Find in files... dialog

If you press the **Find** button now, the editor will open a document listing all the occurrences of javax.activation. It has been found in 10 locations in 9 different files.

Opening the **Find in Files** dialog again and pressing the **Replace** button this time will first ask you whether you want to replace the 10 occurrences in the 9 files. Pressing **Yes** will apply the changes.

While this change is easy, it requires you to enter the values for each row in *Table 3.1*, and do so for every project that you want to migrate. If you are running on Linux or macOS, the next option will be more appealing to you.

Note that this option of migration is available from within your favorite IDE.

Sed

Sed is a standard tool on Linux and macOS operating systems. This streaming editor is not available on the Windows platform, however. If you are working with a Windows operating system, you are advised to use one of the other two conversion options.

The following code is the source code for a small Bash script that will automatically replace all the occurrences of the usage of the Java EE namespace with the Jakarta EE namespace. It is driven by a text file with a comma-separated list of old and new namespaces. It then tells sed to recursively traverse the directory tree, starting at the current directory, and perform the substitution on every file with a Java extension:

```
#!/bin/bash
input="./jee-jakartaee.txt"
while IFS= read -r line
do
  IFS=',' read -r -a array <<< "$line"
  sed  -i -e "s/${array[0]}/${array[1]}/g" $(find./ -name *.java)
done < "$input"
```

There are two things to keep in mind. Firstly, it is best to place this script in the root of the `cargotracker` directory. Secondly, the `jee-jakartaee.txt` input file needs to be in the same directory. Both can be downloaded from the **GitHub** project accompanying this book – more precisely, here: `https://github.com/PacktPublishing/Cloud-Native-Development-and-Migration-to-Jakarta-EE`.

Using a specialized plugin for your IDE

So far, you have been shown two options for migrating your sources. We will now show a third one – one that is available from an IDE. In this situation, we are talking about IntelliJ Ultimate Edition. Refactoring is a common functionality in modern IDEs and IntelliJ is no exception. In fact, this migration option lets you trigger very specifically what you want to convert and what not. And even more conveniently, it has a **Java EE** to **Jakarta EE** migration predefined.

You need to have your project imported and opened in IntelliJ. Then, perform the following steps:

1. Select the **Refactor** menu option.

2. From the dropdown, select **Migrate Packages and Classes**.

3. Select **Java EE to Jakarta EE**.

   The following dialog appears:

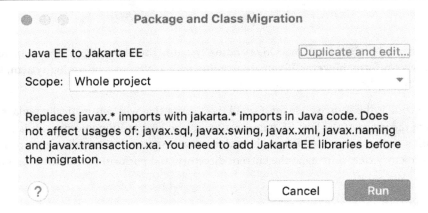

Figure 3.2 – Migration dialog in IntelliJ

4.   Select the **Whole project** option.

5.   Press the **Run** button.

IntelliJ will show a summary of all the occurrences grouped by package name. You can inspect the changes by clicking on the tree in the dialog shown next.

Figure 3.3 – Overview of files to migrate

6.   Finally, press **Do Refactor** to apply the changes.

Once completed, the editor will report `308 occurrences changed`.

While Intellij Ultimate does a great job at changing the namespaces of the imports, it fails to recognize the `javax` usages inside Strings and XML files. To fix this shortcoming, we have to fix some files by hand or by using one of the previous methods.

`RejectedRegistrationAttemptsConsumer`, `MisdirectedCargoConsumer`, `HandlingEventRegistrationAttemptConsumer`, `DeliveredCargoConsumer`, and `CargoHandledConsumer` all use an annotation that uses the name `javax` inside the property value. This annotation looks as follows:

```
@ActivationConfigProperty(propertyName = "destinationType",
propertyValue = "javax.jms.Queue")
```

This activation configuration won't work because of `javax` inside `propertyValue`. To fix this issue, change the annotation to the following example, which uses `jakarta`:

```
@ActivationConfigProperty(propertyName = "destinationType",
propertyValue = "jakarta.jms.Queue"
```

We also need to make changes inside `web.xml` because IntelliJ did not make any changes to this file. Inside the `web.xml` file, the `javax` name is used for the `java.faces` context parameters. In the top part of the `web.xml` file, you can see the `javax` namespace being used. This looks as follows:

```
<context-param>
  <param-name>javax.faces.PROJECT_STAGE</param-name>
  <param-value>Development</param-value>
</context-param>
<context-param>
  <param-name>javax.faces.CLIENT_WINDOW_MODE</param-name>
  <param-value>url</param-value>
</context-param>
```

These context parameters also need to be changed to the new `jakarta` namespace. To do this, you have to replace the `javax` part of the classpath with `jakarta`. The result looks as follows:

```
<context-param>
  <param-name>jakarta.faces.PROJECT_STAGE</param-name>
  <param-value>Development</param-value>
</context-param>
<context-param>
  <param-name>jakarta.faces.CLIENT_WINDOW_MODE</param-name>
  <param-value>url</param-value>
</context-param>
```

With these changes made, the javax name is replaced with jakarta inside the entire project. The last thing to do is upgrade the POM file and dependencies before you can run the project again.

Upgrading your pom.xml file

There is still one more change we need to apply to our code base. We need to tell it that we are now using the Jakarta EE 9 APIs. This is done by updating the dependency in our pom.xml file.

Open the pom.xml file and locate the dependency section. It should look like this:

```
<dependency>
  <groupId>javax</groupId>
  <artifactId>javaee-api</artifactId>
  <version>${javaee_api.version}</version>
  <scope>provided</scope>
</dependency>
```

Now, change it to the following:

```
<dependency>
  <groupId>jakarta.platform</groupId>
  <artifactId>jakarta.jakartaee-api</artifactId>
  <version>9.0.0</version>
  <scope>provided</scope>
</dependency>
```

You have now told Maven that it should use the new Jakarta EE 9 dependencies.

Now, go ahead and rebuild the application by invoking mvn clean install.

Migrating dependencies

With the migration from **Java EE** to the **Jakarta EE** namespace, we need to update three dependencies that the project uses. In this section, we will look into how to upgrade the Java version of the project, the **Payara** application server, and the **PrimeFaces** dependency.

Upgrading the project

To change the Java version Maven uses, we need to make two changes in the pom.xml file. Inside the pom.xml file located in the root of the project directory, you can find the source and target Maven uses for the cargo tracker application.

Currently, the project uses Java version 7, and inside the `pom.xml` file, you can find the following two lines that confirm this:

```
<maven.compiler.source>1.7</maven.compiler.source>
<maven.compiler.target>1.7</maven.compiler.target>
```

We upgraded the cargo tracker application to the latest **long-term support** (**LTS**) version of Java currently available, which is 17. To upgrade the project, replace `1.7` with `17` so it looks like the following:

```
<maven.compiler.source>17</maven.compiler.source>
<maven.compiler.target>17</maven.compiler.target>
```

It's important that you now also change the `JAVA_HOME` system variable that you set in *Chapter 2*. Before you continue, download the Java 17 SDK and set it as the `JAVA_HOME` system variable. If you do not do this, the project won't be able to compile.

Next up is upgrading the Payara application server to the latest version. Upgrading Payara takes two steps. We need to upgrade the Cargo plugin to a version that supports Payara version 6, and we need to upgrade Payara from 4 to 6.

To upgrade Cargo, we need to change the version number from `1.8.1` to `1.10.5`. To do this, change the following line:

```
<cargo.version>1.8.1</cargo.version>
```

The result should look like this:

```
<cargo.version>1.10.5</cargo.version>
```

Upgrading the Payara application server

We have changed the version of the cargo plugin used at the bottom of the `pom.xml` file. The next step is to change the Payara container ID and download URI. We are moving from Payara 4 to 6; to do this, change the following lines:

```
<cargo.payara.container_id>glassfish4x</cargo.payara.container_id>
<cargo.payara.download_uri>https://repo1.maven.org/maven2/fish/payara/
distributions/payara/6.2023.2/payara-6.2023.2.zip</cargo.payara.
download_uri>
```

Change them to look like the following example:

```
<cargo.payara.container_id>glassfish6x</cargo.payara.container_id>
<cargo.payara.download_uri>https://repo1.maven.org/maven2/fish/payara/
distributions/payara/6.2023.2/payara-6.2023.2.zip</cargo.payara.
download_uri>
```

The `glassfish6x` container ID tells the cargo plugin what version of Payara we want to use. Cargo uses the download URI to download a version of Payara. To finish the Cargo upgrade, we need to update the `artifact` ID defined inside the plugin. At the bottom of the `pom.xml` file, you will find the Cargo plugin. We need to take this artifact ID:

```
<artifactId>cargo-maven2-plugin</artifactId>
```

And we need to change it into this one:

```
<artifactId>cargo-maven3-plugin</artifactId>
```

This finishes the Payara and Cargo upgrade to the latest version.

The Cargo tracker uses **Derby** as an in-memory database to store cargo information, but this is no longer possible if we want to use Payara 6. Payara has replaced Derby with **H2** for several reasons. This means that we must change the data source inside the `web.xml` file.

Inside `web.xml`, we need to replace the data source that looks as follows with one that uses H2:

```
<data-source>
    <name>java:app/jdbc/CargoTrackerDatabase</name>
    <class-name>org.apache.derby.jdbc.EmbeddedDriver</class-name>
    <url>jdbc:derby:${webapp.databaseTempDir}
        /cargo-tracker-database;create=true</url>
</data-source>
```

To use H2, we need to replace the class name to tell Payara which driver to use to connect the database. The URL tells Payara where to find the database, and `:mem:` tells H2 that we want to use an in-memory database. The last parameter is the name of the database that H2 has to create:

```
<data-source>
    <name>java:app/jdbc/CargoTrackerDatabase</name>
    <class-name>org.h2.Driver</class-name>
    <url>jdbc:h2:mem:cargo-tracker-database</url>
</data-source
```

Upgrading PrimeFaces

The last dependency we need to upgrade is **PrimeFaces**. This upgrade also consists of two steps: upgrading the dependency to the latest version and changing the PrimeFaces theme because the theme used by the project is no longer supported.

To upgrade the `primefaces` dependency, we need to change the version and add a classifier.

The current `primefaces` dependency looks like the following:

```
<dependency>
    <groupId>org.primefaces</groupId>
    <artifactId>primefaces</artifactId>
    <version>8.0</version>
</dependency>
```

With the upgrade, it should look like the following example. We changed the version to `10.0.0` and added the `jakarta` classifier:

```
<dependency>
    <groupId>org.primefaces</groupId>
    <artifactId>primefaces</artifactId>
    <version>10.0.0</version>
    <classifier>jakarta</classifier>
</dependency>
```

As mentioned earlier, we need to change the theme. To do this, go to the `web.xml` file and look for the following lines at the top part of the file:

```
<context-param>
    <param-name>primefaces.THEME</param-name>
    <param-value>omega</param-value>
</context-param>
```

The `param-value` tells PrimeFaces we want to use the `omega` theme for the project. This theme is not usable with version 10 of PrimePaces. To switch to a different theme, change the previous code line into this:

```
<context-param>
    <param-name>primefaces.THEME</param-name>
    <param-value>saga</param-value>
</context-param>
```

After performing the last step, we concluded the migration from `javax` to `jakarta`. You can now run `mvn clean` and `mvn package cargo:run` to run the Cargo tracker application using Jakarta EE on Payara 6.

Red Hat MTA

MTA, which stands for **Migration Toolkit for Applications**, can automatically convert your Java EE projects to Jakarta EE. It does so by applying a certain set of rules. MTA is a very extensive product. Conversions can be done via the following:

- A user interface
- Command-line tools
- An OpenShift operator
- IDE plugins

Before you can use MTA, you need to download (`https://developers.redhat.com/products/mtr/download`) and install it. For installation instructions, we refer you to the official documentation (`https://access.redhat.com/documentation/en-us/migration_toolkit_for_applications/6.2/html/cli_guide/index?extIdCarryOver=true&sc_cid=701f2000001Css5AAC`). You should install the command-line tools, as those will be the ones you will need for executing migrations on your machine.

Once you have the command-line tools installed, you can start migrating. We will again use the IntelliJ plugin to execute the migration. You need to install the MTA plugin from the **Plugins** page:

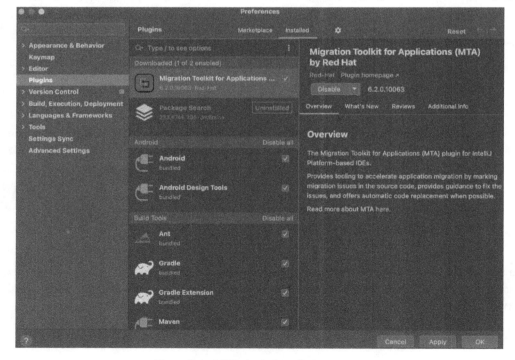

Figure 3.4 – MTA plugin installation screen

Once the plugin is installed, you will have a new tab in your UI labeled **Migration Toolkit for Applications**. Follow these steps:

1. Click on the tab.

    There should be a default configuration entry in the list.

    If not, right-click and choose **New Configuration**.

    Your screen should now look like this:

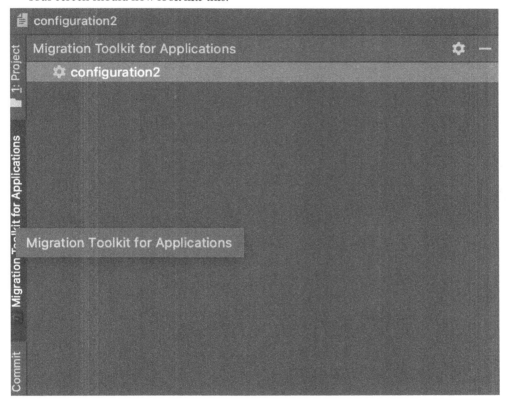

Figure 3.5 – Configuration entry in the MTA plugin

2. Double-click the configuration.

3. Enter the information as shown in the following figure (note that we selected **Windup Configuration** at the bottom).

4. Make sure you enter the location where you installed the command-line tools for MTA.

5. Close the configuration.

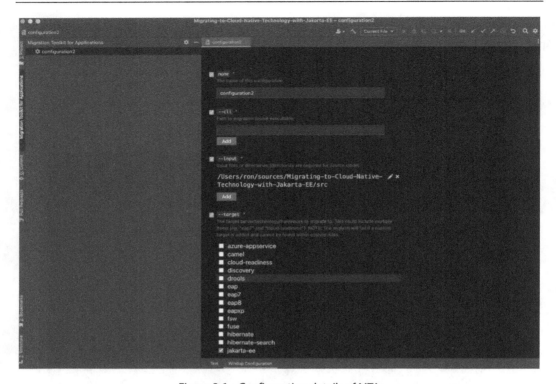

Figure 3.6 – Configuration details of MTA

6. Back in the list of configurations, you can now select the configuration you just modified, right-click it, and choose **Run Analysis**:

Figure 3.7 – The Run Analysis pop-up menu option

7. Once the analysis is completed, the configuration in the left panel will be updated with a report and a results section.

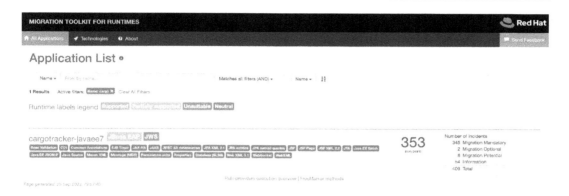

Figure 3.8 – Overview of the migration report

8. Click on the reports to go to the migration report. Next, click on `cargotracker-javaee7`.

9. You will see a summary of your project's artifacts, the type of incidents detected, and even an estimate of required story points to apply the changes.

Figure 3.9 – MTA dashboard main screen

Note that there are several more tabs at the top that can provide excellent information about your application, such as the **Technologies** screen shown here:

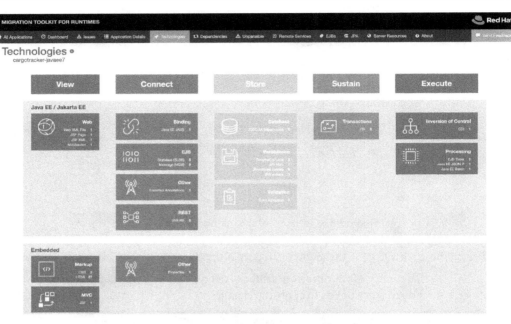

Figure 3.10 – MTA Technologies overview screen

But it does not stop there. If you have executed the analysis against your IntelliJ workspace, specified in the -input parameter, it will show you all the incidents found in your source code.

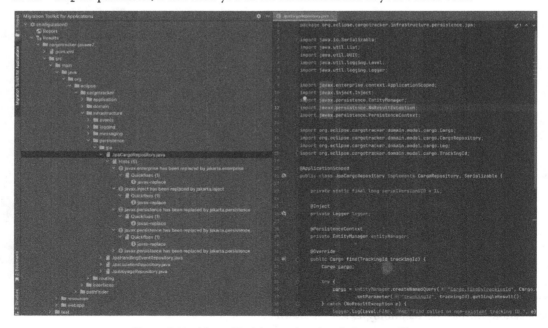

Figure 3.11 – View of incidents related to their source files

If a quick fix can be applied, you can do so by right-clicking the incident and choosing **Apply All Quickfixes**.

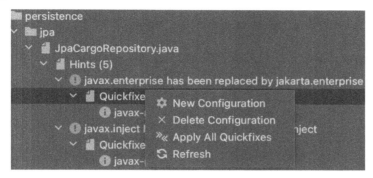

Figure 3.12 – Applying a quick fix

Quick fixes can be applied to a single incident, all incidents in a file, or on increasingly higher levels.

Upgrading your application server

Now, you have your source code upgraded to the Jakarta namespace and updated your dependencies. You have also upgraded to a newer version of your application server.

Should you use a different application server than Payara in your projects, you can use the information in this section to choose the correct version of the application server to use.

There are two versions of Jakarta EE9: Jakarta EE 9 and Jakarta EE 9.1. There is no functional difference between the two; they do not contain distinctive features. However, as the migration was such a huge effort, it was decided that compatibility against Java 11 was only introduced in Jakarta EE 9.1. Thus, if you plan to run your application server on Java 8, a Jakarta EE 9 server will suffice; otherwise, use Jakarta EE 9.1 on Java 11 and higher.

The following table lists some of the more common application servers.

Application server	Jakarta EE 9-compatible	Jakarta EE 9.1-compatible
Eclipse Glassfish	6.0	6.1
Open Liberty	21.0.0.12	21.0.0.12
WildFly	23.0.2	25.0.0
Payara Enterprise Server	6.2021.1	6.2021.1
IBM WebSphere Liberty	21.0.0.12	21.0.0.12

Table 3.2 – Jakarta EE 9 compatible application servers

Summary

In this chapter, you have learned how to migrate the Cargo Tracker application from Java EE to Jakarta EE. You have learned several ways to migrate the code. You have also learned how to upgrade the dependencies of the application. Finally, you have learned which application server version you should choose for running the Cargo Tracker application and your own applications.

These steps are all vitally important for what we are going to cover in the next chapter, which is upgrading the application to leverage the new functionality provided by Jakarta EE 10.

4

Modernizing Your Application with the Latest Features

The application you are migrating, which in our case is the Cargo tracker application, has not been majorly upgraded in the last few years, which has resulted in it missing out on lots of new features and not using features that the cloud has to offer, such as monitoring and scaling. In this chapter, we are going to focus on Jakarta EE 10 and upgrading an application to cloud-native standards. During this chapter, you are going to modernize your application so that it is ready to run in the cloud while using the latest features of Jakarta EE 10.

In this chapter, we are going to cover the following topics:

- The most significant changes made to Jakarta EE 10
- Adding the first cloud-native feature – resilience
- Adding the second cloud-native feature – monitoring
- Using Prometheus and Grafana to visualize the monitoring process

After completing this chapter, you will be able to upgrade your application to one that can use the cloud and the newest features of Jakarta EE 10. You will also know how to monitor the health of your application. This will enable you to keep up with the newest releases of Jakarta EE.

Technical requirements

To follow along with this chapter, you need to have finished *Chapter 3*. For this chapter, it is important to have an application that runs on Jakarta EE 10 or newer but isn't using the new features yet.

The most significant changes to Jakarta EE 10

Jakarta EE 10 is the first edition of Jakarta EE that added functionality since joining the Eclipse Foundation. In this section, we will be going over the most meaningful changes that were made. It is in no sense meant to be an exhaustive overview of all the changes. Neither will we apply these changes to our existing Cargo Tracker application. Making these changes would be very use-case-specific, such as setting up a different authentication mechanism or changing primary keys.

Core Profile

We have already pointed out that one of the major features was adding the Core Profile. This profile targets smaller applications such as microservices. In fact, according to the official documentation, it targets modern cloud applications with a focus on a minimal set of APIs that support microservices with a focus on enabling implementations that make use of **ahead-of-time (AOT)** compilation builds to minimize startup time and memory footprint.

That is quite a sentence, and to fully understand what it means, we are going to break it down. *It targets smaller applications*. That is an interesting observation. In the chapter on the history of Java EE/Jakarta EE, you read that the original profiles targeted two kinds of implementations: web servers and application servers. The web profiles target smaller applications that don't use many specifications, while the full profiles implemented by application servers target larger and more complex applications. These full profile implementations provide a variety of functionality to applications that are being deployed on those servers: EJBs, security, transaction management, and JNDI, to name a few. This is in contrast to the core profile, which targets very precise microservices that do not use a lot of the Jakarta specification.

Moving to smaller applications contrasts with these full-profile implementations. But it does align with the current trend in software architecture, which is that monolithic applications are broken down into smaller applications. So, Jakarta EE wants to be a platform that allows for microservices.

It allows for the creation of modern, cloud-native applications. We've already seen what cloud-native applications all are about. To enable this cloud-nativeness, Jakarta EE and Micro Profile can be used since they complement each other.

Focus on a minimal set of APIs that support microservices. Before the Core Profile arrived, we used the Web Profile to create microservices. But in contrast to the Web Profile, the Core Profile only requires seven specifications to be available:

- Jakarta Annotations
- Jakarta CDI Lite
- Jakarta Dependency Injection
- Jakarta Interceptors

- Jakarta JSON Processing

- Jakarta JSON Binding

- Jakarta RESTful Web Services

Another benefit of only having seven specifications that need to be implemented is that it makes it easier to create a valid application server that complies with the Jakarta EE 10 core profile specification. This allows the community to create more application servers that would better fit their use case.

Then, there is a focus on enabling implementations that make use of AOT compilation. This is quite a different process from the normal JIT compilation that Java runtime uses by default.

Normally, a Java file is compiled into a class file. This is before executing the code. During the execution of the code, the **Java Virtual Machine (JVM)** translates the bytecode into platform-specific machine code. For this, it has two compilers on board, named C1 and C2. C1 quickly produces non-optimized machine code. At some point, a method execution count threshold might be passed, and then the JVM decides that it is time to optimize the generated machine code. This is where the C2 compiler comes in. It will take more time to generate the code, but the generated machine code is highly optimized.

It is important to remember that all this compilation is done during the execution of the application.

AOT compilation, on the other hand, is performed before the application is executed. In a complicated and time-consuming process, the AOT compiler will walk every possible path of execution and generate the required machine code. There are several advantages of this:

- There is no need for a full-fledged JVM when running the application

- The application is already in binary format, so no time is spent at runtime on the compilation

- All classes are known at startup, so no scanning of JAR/WAR/EAR files is required

- Optimized memory consumption

- Quick startup times as everything that needs to start is known upfront

As with so many things, AOT does not come for free. The most notable disadvantages are as follows:

- Extremely long compilation times

- The ability of dynamic class loading is lost

- The generated binary targets a specific platform, losing the idea of writing your code once and running it anywhere

- You lose the ability to optimize code execution at runtime like the C2 compiler does

The most famous AOT compiler right now is GraalVM from Oracle. It comes in both open source and licensed versions. Though the former provides the most features, the latter comes with support and is more optimized.

Using UUIDs as keys

Before looking at how to use **Universally Unique IDentifiers** (**UUIDs**), we should define what they are and why you would want to use them. UUIDs are used to uniquely identify an object or entity. They are defined in RFC-4122.

There are several different types of UUIDs:

- **Type 1**: Date-time and MAC address-based
- **Type 2**: Date-time, MAC address, and **Distributed Computing Environment** (**DCE**)-based
- **Type 3**: MD5 hashing of a namespace and a name
- **Type 4**: Randomly generated numbers
- **Type 5**: SHA-1 hashing of a namespace and a name

Though their name implies that they are always unique, there is a possibility of duplicate values. Though it varies per type, the overall possibility is so low that it can safely be ignored.

Jakarta Persistence can now use UUIDs as key values. UUIDs are mostly unique values. This allows them to be used as values for keys that require uniqueness. Though duplicates can arise, and depending on the chosen type of UUID this possibility might be higher, in practice, it is very unlikely to happen.

Consider the following code, which does just this:

```
@Entity
public class Vehicle {
@Id
@GeneratedValue(strategy = GenerationType.UUID)
private UUID id;
private String license;
private String type;
}
```

The ID of the Vehicle class is of the java.util.UUID type. The UUID generated by GenerationType.UUID is an rfc-4122-compatible UUID.

Multi-part form parameters

Multi-part form data is useful for uploading larger amounts of data, such as a picture or the contents of a file.

While this is quite common behavior for an application, Jakarta EE does not have a standard solution for this in place. Often, developers have to rely on non-portable implementations that come from their application server vendor.

Finally, with Jakarta EE 10, multi-part form parameters are supported out of the box:

```
@POST
@Path("upload/picture")
@Consumes(MediaType.MULTIPART_FORM_DATA)
public Response postImage(@FormParam("userId") String memberId, @
FormParam("image") EntityPart image) {
    String fileName = image.getFileName().
    orElseThrow(NotSupportedException::new);
    InputStream content = image.getContent();
    return Response.ok("image is uploaded").build();
}
```

We need to define that the endpoint consumes `MULTIPART_FORM_DATA`. Next, we need to define the individual form parameters whose content is to be injected into the variables. In the preceding code, `EntityPart` will hold a stream that contains the image data. Even though a string could be used here, the wiser and more scalable solution is to use an input stream to read the data to prevent the image contents from being loaded into the method in one go.

Pure Java Jakarta Faces views

Yup, you read that right! If you would like to programmatically compose your Jakarta Faces views, you now can. You can skip all the scripting parts and use just Java code.

There are various advantages to doing this. When building a view dynamically, you simply loop over your Java class and create components for each field as required. If you want to exclude certain fields from the view, the conditions under which to do so can be written in Java. Finally, event handlers can be simple Java Lambdas – there is no need to use method references via EL expressions.

If you have written Swing code before using Java SE, then the following example may look very familiar:

```
HtmlForm form = components.create(HtmlForm.COMPONENT_TYPE);
body.getChildren().add(form);

HtmlOutputText message = components.create(HtmlOutputText.COMPONENT_
TYPE);
form.getChildren().add(message);

HtmlCommandButton actionButton =
components.create(HtmlCommandButton.COMPONENT_TYPE);
actionButton.addActionListener(
        e -> message.setValue("I was pressed"));
actionButton.setValue("Press");
form.getChildren().add(actionButton);
```

Here, we're creating a simple HTML form in code. We added an `HtmlOutputText` component to the form. Finally, we created and added an `HtmlCommandButton` component. The action listener method of the button receives a Lamba that will be executed when the button is pressed.

Authenticating with OpenID

How do you handle the authentication of your users in your application? The most common way is to provide a dedicated login with a username and password. Once entered, your application will then try to authenticate your users against the information available in your local database or LDAP.

However, users do not always want to create new accounts for every new site they want to visit. This is where OpenID comes in. Imagine that you have a Google account. When visiting site A, you specify that you want to log in with your Google credentials. Site A has no knowledge or ability to verify your Google credentials by itself. So, it relays the authentication to google.com. Once Google has established that you claim who you say you are, this information is returned to site A.

As authenticating with OpenID becomes more and more common, Jakarta Security now supports OpenID via a set of annotations. Let's have a look at an example:

```
@OpenIdAuthenticationDefinition(
providerURI = "https://accounts.google.com",
clientId = "${config.clientId}",
clientSecret = "${config.clientSecret}",
redirectURI = "${baseURL}/callback",
)
@ApplicationScoped
public class GoogleOpenIdSecurityBean {
}
```

`@OpenIdAuthenticationDefinition` takes several configurable parameters. `providerUri` points to the `OpenId` provider – that is, the participant that does the actual authentication. `clientId` and `clientSecret` inform the provider who it is authenticating for. Finally, `redirectUri` contains the callback endpoint for the provider to return to your applications after the authentication has been completed.

Improved concurrency

Jakarta concurrency had a large number of changes in version 10. Two of the most notable are the introduction of the `@Asynchronous` annotation and the ability to configure `ManagedExecutorService`.

While this annotation is available via the Jakarta Enterprise Beans specification, the new annotation has several clear advantages. First off, EJB requires the full Jakarta EE profile to work – this is not available in the Core Profile, for instance.

Secondly, the old annotation uses the default thread pool from the application server, while the new version allows you to specify which thread pool to use if you don't want to use the default thread pool. This can be of enormous benefit as it allows you to use dedicated thread pools for certain groups of tasks.

Here is an example:

```
public class PaymentService {
  @Asynchronous(executor = "java:app/concurrent/OrderExecutorService")
  public CompletableFuture<OrderStatus> processOrder
      (final Order order) {
    try {
      var status = processAvailability(order);
      return CompletableFuture.completedFuture(status);
    } catch (OrderProcessingException ex) {
      throw new CompletionException(ex);
    }
  }
}
```

We simply annotate the method with @Synchronous and optionally specify which executor service is to be used.

Adding the first cloud-native feature – resilience

Adding resilience to your system is not very challenging from a technical point of view. The real challenge lies in deciding where to add resilience to your code and what type of resilience to add. To add resilience to our code, we will use MicroProfile as it complements a Jakarta EE application very nicely.

You can add MicroProfile by adding the following entry to your pom.xml file:

```
<dependency>
    <groupId>org.eclipse.microprofile</groupId>
    <artifactId>microprofile</artifactId>
    <version>5.0</version>
    <type>pom</type>
    <scope>provided</scope>
</dependency>
```

By adding this xml to your pom.xml file, you can start using MicroProfile in your application.

Next, perform the standard steps for building and starting your application. They should not be a surprise to you anymore.

For the CargoTracker application, you need to run the following commands:

- mvn clean install
- mvn cargo:run

With MicroProfile available inside your application, we can use the following options to add resilience to our application:

- `@Timeout`
- `@Retry`
- `@Fallback`
- `@Bulkhead`
- `@CircuitBreaker`
- `@Asynchronous`

As mentioned previously, `@Asynchronous` is a special case, so it will not be handled here. We will provide examples of the other resilience methods here.

`@Timeout` is a resilience method that we would want to add to some call to an operation or another system that is in danger of taking a long time. To prevent the system from becoming unresponsive, we can limit how long we want the operation to run before it is cut off.

An ideal location in our code to use the `@Timeout` option is the graph traversal code. It is located in the `ExternalRoutingService` class. There, the `fetchRoutesForSpecification` method performs a web client call to retrieve route specifications.

Technically, it might be possible that the external system is slow to respond, or worse, unavailable.

To limit the impact this will have on our system, we can add the `@Timeout` annotation. The code will now look this:

```
@Timeout(value = 2000)
public List<Itinerary> fetchRoutesForSpecification(RouteSpecification
routeSpecification) {
```

If the call to the external system fails, it will fail early now thanks to the annotation you've added. But if it fails, would you not like to retry again? After all, it might just be a simple network failure that has caused this. It might be a recoverable error.

To support a retry, will need to add the following code. It will make us wait 250 milliseconds between retries and it will only retry twice as opposed to the default value of 3:

```
@Timeout(value = 2000)
@Retry(maxRetries = 2, delay = 250)
public List<Itinerary> fetchRoutesForSpecification(RouteSpecification
routeSpecification) {
```

Cargo Tracker offers the functionality to change a destination. This will be done from the changeDestination screen. The .xhtml file is backed by a @Named backing bean called ChangeDestination. It offers users a dropdown to select the name of the new location. This dropdown is backed by a list of locations called potentialDestinations. This list is loaded during the bean's initialization. It retrieves the locations via listShippingLocations of BookingServiceFacade. This method does the actual loading by querying the database.

Phew – that was quite a trip! It has shown us how quickly things can become complicated, especially with an application such as Cargo Tracker, which was set up with **domain-driven design** (**DDD**) in mind and where there is a clear distinction between the different architectural layers of the application.

Anyway, if for some reason (yes, network, we are looking at you!) the required values cannot be retrieved, it would be nice to provide a default response. Let's be honest – an empty list with locations is still better than reporting some strange error to the user.

We will annotate listShippingLocatons with a default response via @Fallback.

Have a look at the following code:

```
@Override
@Fallback(fallbackMethod = "shippingLocationsFallback")
public List<org.eclipse.cargotracker.interfaces.booking.facade.dto.
Location> listShippingLocations() {
```

Note that any situation that makes listShippingLocation throw an exception will trigger the fallback method. You can configure this behavior with the applyOn and skipOn parameters.

Next, we need to provide an implementation for the method that is specified in the fallbackMethod parameter.

It will look like this:

```
private List<org.eclipse.cargotracker.interfaces.booking.facade.dto.
Location> listShippingLocationsFallBack() {
    return List.of();
}
```

Note that the fallback method can be private, and in most situations, it should be private to prevent any other class from having unwanted access to this method.

We simply return an empty list here because we have no reasonable alternative values.

Adding the second cloud-native feature – monitoring

So, we have made our application more robust than it was by adding some resilience features. Next, we will go a step further and add monitoring functionality to our application.

The idea behind monitoring is two-fold.

First, it should supply you with information that your system is running as expected. Any errors, exceptions, network failures, database hiccups, and more should be identified, registered, and reported.

Secondly, monitoring should provide you with information about the usage of the system. How many new users do we have, how many orders are there in the system, how often does a certain REST endpoint access, and how often is a critical business method invoked?

The monitoring process consists of several steps:

1.   Add annotations to your code that will actively monitor the metrics.
2.   Expose the metrics data for harvesting.
3.   Harvest the data.
4.   Generate alerts and create visualized data.

In this section, we will discuss the first step and identify what we want to monitor and how to make the required code changes.

Looking at the default metrics of a running system

Out of the box, MicroProfile Metrics already gathers a lot of information when it comes to the state of your application. It defines three categories of information:

1.   System metrics.
2.   Application metrics.
3.   Vendor-specific metrics.

Let's take a look at these metrics. We will use the Cargo Tracker application for this. Navigate to `http://localhost:8080/metrics`; you will see a list of all default metrics. Here is a part of the output:

```
# TYPE base_cpu_availableProcessors gauge
base_cpu_availableProcessors 10
# TYPE base_cpu_systemLoadAverage gauge
base_cpu_systemLoadAverage 5.9248046875
# TYPE base_gc_total_total counter
base_gc_total_total{name="G1 Young Generation"} 54
base_gc_total_total{name="G1 Old Generation"} 0
# TYPE base_jvm_uptime_seconds gauge
base_jvm_uptime_seconds 56.064
# TYPE base_memory_committedHeap_bytes gauge
base_memory_committedHeap_bytes 2.87309824E8
# TYPE base_memory_committedNonHeap_bytes gauge
```

```
base_memory_committedNonHeap_bytes 2.17448448E8
# TYPE base_memory_maxHeap_bytes gauge
base_memory_maxHeap_bytes 5.36870912E8
# TYPE base_memory_maxNonHeap_bytes gauge
base_memory_maxNonHeap_bytes -1
# TYPE base_memory_usedHeap_bytes gauge
base_memory_usedHeap_bytes 2.28326272E8
```

Note that for brevity, we left out the #HELP lines.

Some of these metrics might be quite useful as they allow you to monitor the behavior and health of your system. This data is very important for teams who have to support the application while it is in production. The metrics can be the number of processors, the average load of the processors, the number of garbage collections, the uptime, and several memory statistics. The latter might come in handy as a way of determining memory leaks in your application.

At the end of the output, we can see a vendor-specific metric:

```
# TYPE vendor_system_cpu_load gauge
vendor_system_cpu_load 0.08853118712273642
```

Adding metrics to your system

Next, we are going to add some metrics of our own to the Cargo Tracker application. The first step is to identify which metrics you or your stakeholder might be interested in. The tech department will likely be very interested in metrics that can help verify that the system is working as expected. The business stakeholders, on the other hand, might be more interested in some business-oriented key performance indicators. In this section, we are going to add some of both types to our application.

Recall *Chapter 2*, where we introduced the Cargo Tracker application, which has one REST endpoint to retrieve information about existing shipments. That endpoint can be reached at http://localhost:8080/cargo-tracker/rest/cargo and will show a list of outstanding shipments.

Here is part of the output:

```
{
"trackingId": "ABC123",
"routingStatus": "ROUTED",
"misdirected": false,
"transportStatus": "IN_PORT",
"atDestination": false,
"origin": "CNHKG",
"lastKnownLocation": "USNYC"
},
{
```

```
"trackingId": "JKL567",
"routingStatus": "ROUTED",
"misdirected": true,
"transportStatus": "ONBOARD_CARRIER",
"atDestination": false,
"origin": "CNHGH",
"lastKnownLocation": "USNYC"
},
```

We might be interested in how often this endpoint is being invoked. To set up metrics for this, we need to change the code in the `CargoMonitorService` class, as follows:

```
@GET
@Produces(MediaType.APPLICATION_JSON)
@Counted(name="getAllCargo", absolute = true)
public JsonArray getAllCargo() {
```

Here, we added the `@Counted` annotation. We have named the metric `getAllCargo`. By specifying `absolute=true`, the metric will be registered in the output as `application_getAllCargo`. When we set `absolute` to `false`, the full package path and class name will be prepended to the given name.

Let's fire a few HTTP requests to the REST endpoint (`http://localhost:8080/cargo-tracker/rest/cargo`) to invoke the method several times. Then, when we invoke the metrics endpoint again via `http://localhost:8080/metrics`, we should see that an entry has been added at the bottom, like this:

```
# TYPE application_getAllCargo_total counter
application_getAllCargo_total 3
```

Another useful metric involves determining how long a method is running. For this, we can use the `@Timed` annotation.

We will apply this metric to the same method, so it will look like this:

```
@GET
@Produces(MediaType.APPLICATION_JSON)
@Counted(name="getAllCargo", absolute = false)
@Timed(name = "getAllCargoTiming", absolute = false, tags =
{"type=performance"})
public JsonArray getAllCargo() {
```

Note that we are storing the information for the metrics under `getAllCargoTiming` and that we are also adding a selector key/value pair. This will enable us to make more precise selections on the resulting data.

Go and invoke the specified method by accessing `http://localhost:8080/cargo-tracker/rest/cargo` and then retrieve the new metrics.

These should look something like this:

```
# TYPE application_org_eclipse_cargotracker_interfaces_booking_rest_
CargoMonitoringService_getAllCargoTiming_rate_per_second gauge
application_org_eclipse_cargotracker_interfaces_booking_rest_
CargoMonitoringService_getAllCargoTiming_rate_per_second{_app="cargo-
tracker",type="performance"} 0.14885107622981664
# TYPE application_org_eclipse_cargotracker_interfaces_booking_rest_
CargoMonitoringService_getAllCargoTiming_one_min_rate_per_second gauge
application_org_eclipse_cargotracker_interfaces_booking_rest_
CargoMonitoringService_getAllCargoTiming_one_min_rate_per_second{_
app="cargo-tracker",type="performance"} 0.2
# TYPE application_org_eclipse_cargotracker_interfaces_booking_rest_
CargoMonitoringService_getAllCargoTiming_five_min_rate_per_second
gauge
application_org_eclipse_cargotracker_interfaces_booking_rest_
CargoMonitoringService_getAllCargoTiming_five_min_rate_per_second{_
app="cargo-tracker",type="performance"} 0.2
# TYPE application_org_eclipse_cargotracker_interfaces_booking_rest_
CargoMonitoringService_getAllCargoTiming_fifteen_min_rate_per_second
gauge
application_org_eclipse_cargotracker_interfaces_booking_rest_
CargoMonitoringService_getAllCargoTiming_fifteen_min_rate_per_second{_
app="cargo-tracker",type="performance"} 0.2
# TYPE application_org_eclipse_cargotracker_interfaces_booking_rest_
CargoMonitoringService_getAllCargoTiming_mean_seconds gauge
application_org_eclipse_cargotracker_interfaces_booking_rest_
CargoMonitoringService_getAllCargoTiming_mean_seconds{_app="cargo-
tracker",type="performance"} 0.006363875
# TYPE application_org_eclipse_cargotracker_interfaces_booking_rest_
CargoMonitoringService_getAllCargoTiming_max_seconds gauge
application_org_eclipse_cargotracker_interfaces_booking_rest_
CargoMonitoringService_getAllCargoTiming_max_seconds{_app="cargo-
tracker",type="performance"} 0.006363875
# TYPE application_org_eclipse_cargotracker_interfaces_booking_rest_
CargoMonitoringService_getAllCargoTiming_min_seconds gauge
application_org_eclipse_cargotracker_interfaces_booking_rest_
CargoMonitoringService_getAllCargoTiming_min_seconds{_app="cargo-
tracker",type="performance"} 0.006363875
# TYPE application_org_eclipse_cargotracker_interfaces_booking_rest_
CargoMonitoringService_getAllCargoTiming_stddev_seconds gauge
application_org_eclipse_cargotracker_interfaces_booking_rest_
CargoMonitoringService_getAllCargoTiming_stddev_seconds{_app="cargo-
tracker",type="performance"} 0
# TYPE application_org_eclipse_cargotracker_interfaces_booking_rest_
CargoMonitoringService_getAllCargoTiming_seconds summary
application_org_eclipse_cargotracker_interfaces_booking_rest_
```

```
CargoMonitoringService_getAllCargoTiming_seconds_sum{_app="cargo-
tracker",type="performance"} 0.006363875
application_org_eclipse_cargotracker_interfaces_booking_rest_
CargoMonitoringService_getAllCargoTiming_seconds{_app="cargo-tracker",
type="performance",quantile="0.5"} 0.006363875
application_org_eclipse_cargotracker_interfaces_booking_rest_
CargoMonitoringService_getAllCargoTiming_seconds{_app="cargo-tracker",
type="performance",quantile="0.75"} 0.006363875
application_org_eclipse_cargotracker_interfaces_booking_rest_
CargoMonitoringService_getAllCargoTiming_seconds{_app="cargo-tracker",
type="performance",quantile="0.95"} 0.006363875
application_org_eclipse_cargotracker_interfaces_booking_rest_
CargoMonitoringService_getAllCargoTiming_seconds{_app="cargo-tracker",
type="performance",quantile="0.98"} 0.006363875
application_org_eclipse_cargotracker_interfaces_booking_rest_
CargoMonitoringService_getAllCargoTiming_seconds{_app="cargo-tracker",
type="performance",quantile="0.99"} 0.006363875
application_org_eclipse_cargotracker_interfaces_booking_rest_
CargoMonitoringService_getAllCargoTiming_seconds{_app="cargo-tracker",
type="performance",quantile="0.999"} 0.006363875
```

As you can see, you are getting quite a large set of values for just the one metric we've specified.

Using Prometheus and Grafana to visualize the monitoring process

With the metrics enabled, we now have a big list of lines that tell us how the system is behaving and what resources the application is using. While this gives you a window into the application tracker, the data is not very clear. You can't see at a glance if the system is healthy or if some metrics are entering the red zone and are (almost) at their maximum.

To make these metrics more readable so that you can see what is happening inside the system, we are going to set up a dashboard. To create a dashboard, we need two components: Prometheus and Grafana. We will use Prometheus to pull the metrics from the application, store them, and make the data queryable. We will use Grafana to create the actual dashboard that is going to show the metrics.

By doing this, the metrics will be pulled from the application by Prometheus, and Grafana will query Prometheus for the metric data and show it in a dashboard.

Setting up Prometheus

Prometheus is an open source system for monitoring and alerting. The project started in 2012 at SoundCloud. At the time of writing, many developers use it to collect metrics from their applications and store them inside Prometheus. It also offers multiple ways to query the data that is stored inside it using PromQL.

Prometheus uses a pull mechanism to collect metrics from the applications it monitors. This has a few benefits, such as knowing if an application is down in advance. In the previous section, you set up an endpoint that Prometheus can use to pull metrics from.

Setting up Docker Compose

We are going to use Docker to run an instance of Prometheus. To do so, we need to alter the already existing Docker Compose file so that we can add a Prometheus service.

Inside the Docker Compose file, add the following lines:

```
prometheus:
  image: bitnami/prometheus:latest
  ports:
    - "9090:9090"
```

The first line in the previous example is the name of the service we want to create. In this case, it is Prometheus. Then, we have to define the image that belongs to this service. Here, we are using the latest Prometheus image built by Bitnami. The last thing we need to define is some ports so that we can connect to the instance once it is running. We have chosen to port forward from 9000 to 9000. When you run this code, you will have a running instance of Prometheus, but it won't start collecting metrics out of nowhere. If you go to localhost:9000, you will see an empty Prometheus instance that has no data to query. To fix this, in the next section, we are going to create a job that will collect data.

Setting up the Prometheus settings

The first time you start up docker-compose, you will see an empty Prometheus instance that does not collect or have any metrics. This is fine if you only want to try some things out. If you delete the container of the Prometheus instance, you will have to start again, and that can be quite some work to undertake if you delete your containers often. The same also goes when you have a colleague who wants to have the same setup as you have. Your colleague will have to set up their Prometheus instance the same as you have. This also becomes tedious if you have to do this for your entire team and each environment you want a Prometheus service to run in, such as test, acceptance, and production.

To fix this the first thing you have to do is create a directory inside the project that can hold the settings file. We've created a directory directly inside the project folder. The complete path looks like this: cargo-tracker/prometheus. Inside the Prometheus instance, you need to create a file for the configuration; we chose to name this file prometheus.yml. This is going to be a YAML file that specifies some global settings and settings for the scrape job we want Prometheus to perform on the cargo-tracker application.

Inside the `prometheus.yml` file, you need to place the following configuration:

```
global:
  scrape_interval:       10s



  external_labels:
    monitor: 'payara5-monitor'



scrape_configs:
  - job_name: 'payara5'
    scrape_interval: 2s
    metrics_path: '/metrics'
    static_configs:
      - targets: ['cargo-tracker-app:8080']
```

This configuration creates a scrape configuration for Prometheus to use. This tells Prometheus the following things:

- The name of the job
- How often it should scrape the given metrics
- The path to the metrics on the target
- The targets for the scraping

In the previous section, you could see the metrics of `cargo-tracker` at `localhost:8080/metrics`. You will have to do the same to let Prometheus know where it can find the metrics. Because we're using `docker-compose`, we do not have to use localhost; we can use the service names instead. Inside `docker-compose` from the previous chapters, we had a service called `cargo-tracker`. We can use that name inside the job configuration and Docker will resolve that to an actual address that the Prometheus instance can use. Using the service name, we can specify the target application like this: `cargo-tracker-app:8080`. The complete URL that Prometheus will use will be `cargo-tracker-app:8080/metrics`.

With the configuration file ready, you need to add a single line to the `docker-compose` file. We made a configuration file but we did not tell Prometheus to use it, so we need to make this file available inside the container. To do that, we need to mount the `prometheus.yml` file, which we can do by running the `volume` keyword inside the `docker-compose` file, like this:

```
volumes:
 - ./prometheus/prometheus.yml:/opt/bitnami/prometheus/conf/
prometheus.yml
```

With this line added, the configuration will be available to Prometheus. The complete `docker-compose` will look as follows:

```
version: "3.9"
services:
 cargo-tracker-app:
   build: .
   ports:
     - "4848:4848"
     - "8080:8080"
     - "8181:8181"
     - "9009:9009"
 prometheus:
   image: bitnami/prometheus:latest
   volumes:
     - ./prometheus/prometheus.yml:/opt/bitnami/prometheus/conf
       /prometheus.yml
   ports:
     - "9090:9090"
```

Now that the configuration file and `docker-compose` are ready, we can start the docker-compose file and see if it works. In your browser, go to `http://localhost:9090/config`. Here, you can see the configuration of the Prometheus instance. If everything works, you should see the following output:

Figure 4.1 – Configuration in Prometheus

Setting up Grafana

Grafana is a tool for querying and visualizing the data we get from the metrics in dashboards that we create. Creating a dashboard has the advantage of displaying data so that the user can see the status of the system. If certain metrics are at 100% or at 0%, it may be a signal something is wrong and needs fixing. This is easier to see with a dashboard than using raw metrics.

Setting up docker-compose

In this section, we are going to run Grafana inside a container, just like we did with Prometheus. To do this, we need to change the `docker-compose` file again. We need to add a new service for Grafana. The following example shows how we can add the new service using the latest Grafana image from Grafana:

```
grafana:
  image: grafana/grafana:latest
  ports:
    - "3000:3000"
```

This service will create a Grafana container that has port `3000` port forwarded to port `3000` on the host machine.

When you visit `http://localhost:3000/login`, you will see the login screen of Grafana:

Figure 4.2 – Grafana login screen

You can log in by using `admin` as the username and `admin` as the password. Once you've logged in, you'll be asked to change the password. You can do this or just skip this step to go straight to the welcome screen:

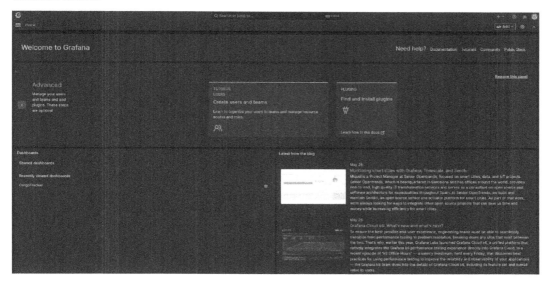

Figure 4.3 – Grafana overview

Within this screen, you can add your data sources and create dashboards. The data sources and dashboards you create will be saved inside the container; others will not be able to see them when they run the `docker-compose` file on their machine. To fix this, we need to store the configuration inside the project and mount it at a later point. To configure Grafana, we need to create three files:

- A configuration file telling it what data sources there are and how to connect to them
- A configuration file telling Grafana where it can find the dashboard
- The dashboard itself

Setting up the auto data source

The first step is to set up a configuration file that we can use to tell Grafana where it can find the metrics. To do this, you need to create a series of directories inside the project. You will need to create this path inside the project directory – that is, `grafana/provisioning/datasources/`.

We will mount this path inside the container later. Inside the data sources directory, create a file named `automatic.yml`. You will use this file to store the data source configuration. The complete path will be `grafana/provisioning/datasources/automatic.yml`. Make sure you put the following configuration inside the YAML file. This configuration tells Grafana the following things:

- The name of the data source
- The access type
- The URL where it can find the resource
- If this is the default data source to use:

```
datasources:
  - name: Prometheus
    access: proxy
    type: prometheus
    url: http://prometheus:9090
    isDefault: true
```

With the data source set up, we can start importing dashboards into Grafana.

Setting up the dashboard so that it loads automatically

If you create a dashboard inside the Grafana constrainer, every time you destroy the container and start it back up, your dashboards will disappear and not be there anymore. This isn't ideal, especially if you're sharing the project with your colleagues as they will have no dashboard at all. The easiest way to share the dashboard and have it available every time you create a new Grafana container is to make it part of the project. Making it part of the project and passing it to the container makes it available every time you create a new container or to any colleague you share the project with.

Making a dashboard part of the project and passing it to the Grafana container is done in two steps. We need to make a YAML file that specifies where Grafana can find the dashboards and we need to create a dashboard to hold the dashboards that we are going to create.

The first step is creating the YAML file to specify the directory of the dashboards. First, you must create a directory to store a YAML file. We created the following directory structure to store this YAML file: `grafana/provisioning/dashboards/`. Inside the `dashboards` directory, you need to create a file named `local.yml`. You are going to use this file to store the configuration. Inside this file, you need to have the following piece of configuration:

```
apiVersion: 1
providers:
  - name: 'default'
```

```
org_id: 1
folder: ''
type: 'file'
options:
  folder: '/var/lib/grafana/dashboards'
```

The first line inside the configuration specifies the version of the configuration, which in this case is going to be 1. After the version, we have to specify the providers; this is going to tell Grafana where it can find the dashboards. The most important option is on the last line. This line specifies the directory inside the container where the dashboard is going to be stored.

The next step is to create a dashboard and store it inside a directory that is inside the project directory. We chose to store the dashboards for `cargo-tracker` inside the `grafana/mydashboards/` directory. Inside the `mydashboards` directory, we created a JSON file called `CargoTracker-1684667357857.json` that will hold the configuration. The next step is to have a dashboard inside this JSON file. We have already created a dashboard for you, so you do not have to do this. The entire JSON file that creates the dashboard is too big to place in this book. Please look at the file on GitHub at `https://github.com/PacktPublishing/Cloud-Native-Development-and-Migration-to-Jakarta-EE/blob/chapter-4-fix/grafana/mydashboards/CargoTracker-1684667357857.json`.

The JSON configuration creates a dashboard inside Grafana that will use the Prometheus data source that you created earlier in this chapter and will display some data from it to the dashboard, as you will see shortly.

Showing Grafana Docker

With the configuration for the dashboard and the dashboard itself created, we need to add them to the container. To do this, you need to add the last two lines of the following example to the Grafana service inside your Docker file:

```
grafana:
  image: grafana/grafana:latest
  ports:
    - "3000:3000"
  volumes:
    - ./grafana/provisioning:/etc/grafana/provisioning
    - ./grafana/mydashboards:/var/lib/grafana/dashboards
```

These two lines will pass the directories you created to the container, making them available for Grafana to read from.

Showing the complete Docker file

The complete Docker file will look as follows. If you followed all the steps in this chapter, you will have altered the Cargo Tracker application so that it includes metrics. Create a Prometheus and Grafana service that will load their configuration from the `cargo-tracker` application:

```
version: "3.9"
services:
  cargo-tracker-app:
    build: .
    ports:
      - "4848:4848"
      - "8080:8080"
      - "8181:8181"
      - "9009:9009"
  prometheus:
    image: bitnami/prometheus:latest
    volumes:
      - ./prometheus/prometheus.yml:/opt/bitnami/prometheus/conf/
prometheus.yml
    ports:
      - "9090:9090"
  grafana:
    image: grafana/grafana:latest
    ports:
      - "3000:3000"
    volumes:
      - ./grafana/provisioning:/etc/grafana/provisioning
      - ./grafana/mydashboards:/var/lib/grafana/dashboards
```

Now, when you run `docker compose-up`, three services are going to be created: `cargo-tracker`, Prometheus, and a Grafana service. When you visit your Grafana instance at `http://localhost:3000` and log in using `admin` as the username and `admin` as the password, you will see the following dashboard. These metrics are gathered from the Prometheus instance, which pulls them from the `cargo-tracker` application:

Figure 4.4 – Dashboard in Grafana

The metrics are refreshed every few seconds and allow you to look inside the `cargo-tracker` application and see what is happening inside. In the next chapter, we are going to take the Cargo Tracker application from this chapter and show you what options you have to make this application more testable.

Summary

In this chapter, you learned about the most significant changes to Jakarta EE 10, including what different profiles there are and when they are used. You also learned about some of the new features that Jakarta EE 10 brings to your application and how you can use MicroProfile together with your application to make it more resilient.

Next, you saw how to add monitoring to your application by using Prometheus to store health metrics and Grafana to display them inside a dashboard, making it easier for teams to see what is happening inside their application.

Now that the application has been updated to the latest version, the next step is to make sure the application keeps working by adding tests. The next chapter will cover how you can test your application to ensure that every still works after every change.

5

Making Your Application Testable

The Cargo Tracker application already has unit tests and good test coverage. That doesn't mean that your current project or the next one is the same. It could be the case that your current project doesn't have unit tests or a low test coverage.

Having a low test coverage or not enough unit tests could impose a thread. What if something changes during a migration and no longer works? How are you going to know if something broke? That's when all kinds of different types of tests come in. In this chapter, you will learn how to create different kinds of tests that test different kinds of aspects of your application.

We're going to cover the following main topics:

- The impact of testing on your migration
- Measuring code coverage of the project
- A word about **test-driven development** (TDD)
- How to create unit tests
- How to create integration tests

By the end of the chapter, you should know what kinds of tests there are, when to use them, and how you can create those tests.

Technical requirements

For this chapter, you need to have Docker installed on your system. For a detailed explanation, see *Chapter 6*, in which the complete installation of Docker is covered. We are going to use Docker to spin up instances for the integration tests. The first part of this chapter is doable without Docker; however, to get the most value out of this chapter, it is important to have Docker installed.

You can find all the code examples from this chapter on GitHub: `https://github.com/ PacktPublishing/Cloud-Native-Development-and-Migration-to-Jakarta-EE/ tree/chapter-5`. The repository contains all the examples from this chapter.

The impact of testing on your migration

Tests are a great tool to measure if your migration was a success or if you still need to fix some parts of the project you are migrating. When all the tests are working correctly, it means that all the functionality those tests cover works just as before the migration. There is also the possibility that some tests started failing during the migration, meaning that some parts of the migration broke the functionality.

If the project you are migrating already has enough tests to cover the functionality, you can skim this chapter to see if you see new things you would like to incorporate in your testing strategy or see an alternative way of testing a Java application. To migrate an application, it is not necessary to overhaul the current testing strategy.

If you are migrating a project with little to no tests, adding tests can help you immensely as the test will indicate if the project keeps working. This chapter covers one of many ways to write tests and have test coverage for the project you are migrating. There are a lot more libraries out there that are worth considering for testing your application, such as Arquillian, Jakarta REST client, and MicroProfile REST client.

Measuring code coverage of the project

Having tests is great, but do you know how much of your project is covered by the tests inside the project? That is where test coverage comes in. Test coverage tells you how much production code is covered by tests. This tells you what functionality is covered by tests and what functionality has to be tested manually.

Measuring test coverage is very easy when you use IntelliJ. All you have to do is navigate to a test class. Inside a test class, you can either right-click on the class to run the tests with coverage or you can run the tests with coverage from the menu options, as in the following screenshot:

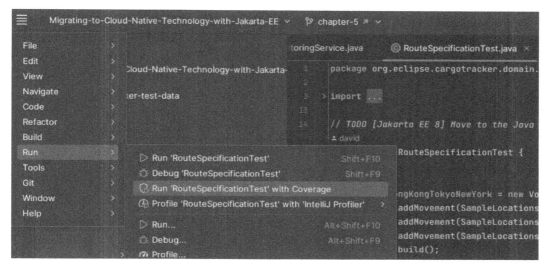

Figure 5.1 – Running tests with coverage

After running the test with coverage, you will see a report that shows you how much of your production code is covered by tests. This is how it will look:

Element ^	Class, %	Method, %	Line, %
org.eclipse.cargotracker.domain.model.c	27% (3/11)	15% (16/106)	14% (42/291)
Cargo	0% (0/1)	0% (0/15)	0% (0/31)
CargoRepository	100% (0/0)	100% (0/0)	100% (0/0)
Delivery	0% (0/2)	0% (0/34)	0% (0/105)
HandlingActivity	0% (0/1)	0% (0/10)	0% (0/32)
Itinerary	50% (1/2)	50% (7/14)	34% (18/52)
Leg	100% (1/1)	36% (4/11)	40% (10/25)
RouteSpecification	100% (1/1)	55% (5/9)	53% (14/26)
RoutingStatus	0% (0/1)	0% (0/3)	0% (0/3)
TrackingId	0% (0/1)	0% (0/7)	0% (0/14)
TransportStatus	0% (0/1)	0% (0/3)	0% (0/3)

Figure 5.2 – Test coverage result

In the previous screenshot, you can see the test coverage for various classes and what percentage of the class is covered. The RouteSpecification class is only covered for 55%. This means that not every method is covered. When you look at the line coverage, you see that only a little more than half the lines are covered.

What percentage of test coverage should you strive for? That depends on many factors. It should be a percentage that you and your team are comfortable with and gives you great confidence that the migrated functionality keeps working. This could be either 60%, 90%, or even 100%. The important thing is that it should help you move forward in your migration and not hold you back.

A word about TDD

A chapter about testing cannot miss a section about TDD. As the name suggests, the test code drives the development of your production code. When you use TDD, you start by creating a test case with, for example, JUnit. In Java, that would look like this:

```
@Test
void goesToNetherlands_success(){
}
```

The last example shows an empty testing method. Here starts the TDD adventure. From here on out, you are not supposed to develop any production while the test succeeds. This means that if we want to develop a new feature, we first need a failing or not compiling test.

The first step could be to create an instance of what you need. This allows you to create a class that you need to hold the business logic. It could be something as simple as the following:

```
@Test
void goesToNetherlands_success(){

RoutingHelper routingHelper = new RoutingHelper();

}
```

If you try to run/compile the project, you will get an exception saying something along the lines of a class or reference is missing or does not exist. That is completely true, and valid because it does not yet exist inside the project. When you are doing TDD, you first want a failing test that you can fix. This is part of the red-green cycle of TDD. You start with a failing test (red) and make it pass (green). To make the test work, all you need to do is create a RoutingHelper class and add it as an import to the test class.

Here's an example of the RoutingHelper class that would make the test compile again:

```
public class RoutingHelper {
}
```

When you added the previous class from the example, you have a working (green) test. The next step would be to make the test fail (red) again. You could do that by adding a method call that you want the RoutingHelper class to have. The next example shows you how this is done by adding a method call inside the testing method:

```
@Test
void goesToNetherlands_success(){
RoutingHelper routingHelper = new RoutingHelper();
routingHelper.goesToNetherlands();

}
```

When you add the method call, the test fails again because the method does not exist yet. Creating this method would be the next step. What we just did was go through the red-green cycle of TDD. We started with a failing test, fixed it, made the test pass, and made it fail again. This is the basis of TDD, and when you develop new features, you want to start with a failing test and try to make it pass. This would be the start of a new red-green cycle. TDD can be applied to any kind of code or test you are writing; this could be a unit test or an integration test. When you use TDD for integration tests, really try to keep the test the execution of the test to be fast, because you are going to execute the test several times.

How to create unit tests

Testing in Java is often done with unit tests. When people talk about test coverage or if you have tests for your code, they most often mean unit tests. Unit testing is a method to test the smallest unit of code. With Java, the smallest unit of code is often a single method. With unit testing, we just test one single method at a time. Sounds simple enough, right? Testing a single method is easy if it doesn't depend on another class, package, database, or even a framework or entire application. That's when unit testing often gets difficult and testing code becomes a huge mess, and nobody wants to touch it anymore. We want to prevent that, so we start at the basics and build our testing strategy up from there, starting with a single unit test.

Tools and libraries required for unit testing

The unit tests that you are going to write in this chapter depend on two very popular testing libraries, JUnit and Mockito. For the unit tests themselves, we are going to use JUnit, and we'll use Mockito to mock any dependencies the code has. These two libraries are very helpful and are almost essential for every project.

JUnit helps you to write the actual unit test. With its built-in annotations, it enables you to mark methods and connect them to different parts of the testing life cycle. A testing life cycle helps you to prepare object instances for your tests. The other essential library is Mockito. Mockito is a library that helps you to create mocks of existing classes in a straightforward way. As you will see later in the examples, mocks are created so that we don't have to interact with real instances of classes and databases.

Creating a unit test

In this section, we will show you how to create a unit test. The Cargo Tracker application is intricate, meaning that you will need some time to fully understand what is going on inside the code. To speed up this process, we are first going to create a method that we can test. This way, you don't have to know any details of the Cargo Tracker application and are able to focus on creating the unit test.

The method we want to use to teach you unit testing needs a class to hold it. Create a class named `RoutingHelper` inside the `org/eclipse/cargotracker/infrastructure/routing` package. Make sure the content of the `RoutingHelper` class looks like this:

```
package org.eclipse.cargotracker.infrastructure.routing;


public class RoutingHelper {
}
```

We can't create unit tests for this because this class does not have any methods inside of it. Let us create one now:

```
boolean goesToNetherlands(RouteSpecification routeSpecification){
  Location destination = routeSpecification.getDestination();
  return "Netherlands".equals(destination.getName());
}
```

This is just a simple method intended to teach you the basics of unit testing. The method in the previous example does only one thing—it checks if the destination of a `RouteSpecification` instance is equal to `Netherlands`. If the location equals the Netherlands, it returns `true`; if it is not the same, it will return `false`.

Let's create a test class for the `RoutingHelper` class. Every class resides inside a directory structure. For the `RoutingHelper` class, this is `src/main/java/org/eclipse/cargotracker/infrastructure/routing/RoutingHelper.java`. It is common for tests to reside inside the test package but with the same directory structure.

The next step is to create a test class that will be used to hold the unit tests for this class. Create a file named `RoutingHelperTest` inside this directory structure: `src/test/java/org/eclipse/cargotracker/infrastructure/routing/RoutingHelperTest.java`. Notice the second directory inside both paths. The production code resides inside the main package, and the test code lives in the test package. This makes it easy to tell them apart, and you won't accidentally call the testing code from your production code.

Make sure the content of the `RoutingHelperTest` class looks like the following:

```
package org.eclipse.cargotracker.infrastructure.routing;
import static org.junit.jupiter.api.Assertions.*;
class RoutingHelperTest {
}
```

With the test class made, we are ready to build the first unit test. Let's start with just an empty method called `goesToNetherlands_success`. We give the test method the same name as the method that it tests and add an underscore and the expected behavior. This tells us what the method tests and what the expected result is going to be without having to read how the method works. The first unit test will look like this:

```
@Test
void goesToNetherlands_success(){

}
```

Every unit test is marked with the `@Test` annotation. This tells JUnit which methods are test methods and which are not. The next step is to test your `goesToNetherlands` method. Inside the test, we will use the `given`, `when`, `then` structure. The `given` part tells the reader what the basis is of the test and which instances the test requires. The `when` part invokes the production code. Inside the `then` part, we verify if what has happened was correct.

For our first unit test, we need to create a `RouteSpecification` class in the `given` part. In the `when` part, we call the `goesToNetherlands` method with the `RouteSpecification` class we created in the `given` part. In the last part of the test method, we are going to verify if what happened was correct.

The resulting unit test will look like the following:

```
@Test
void goesToNetherlands_success(){

  // given
  Location locationNetherlands = new Location(new UnLocode("XXXXX"),
"Netherlands");
  Location locationGermany = new Location(new
UnLocode("OOOOO"),"Germany");
  RouteSpecification routeSpecification = new
RouteSpecification(locationGermany, locationNetherlands, Date.
from(Instant.now()));

  RoutingHelper routingHelper = new RoutingHelper();

  // when
  boolean goesToNetherlands = routingHelper.
goesToNetherlands(routeSpecification);

  // then
  Assertions.assertTrue(goesToNetherlands);
}
```

Here, we create two locations, a route specification, and a routing helper in the `given` part and use both in the remaining part of the unit test.

When you add this code to the application tracker project, your first unit test is done. All you need to do now is run the unit test.

How to create integration tests

In this section, we are going to show you how to create integration tests. The applications we built today are not siloed anymore. Instead, the applications we develop in our day-to-day lives have lots of dependencies on internal and or even external systems. These dependencies all have their own versions, interfaces, and so on that need to keep working when we replace just a small or even a big piece of our application. It is important to know if your application still works after, for example, upgrading a software dependency, server, or operating system.

In the next sections, we are going to walk you through what integration tests are and how you can use them to test your application.

What are integration tests?

To verify if your system still works, you need tests! With unit tests, we only test a small unit of code, not packages, modules, or even entire applications. They are not built with that in mind. To verify that bigger parts or entire applications work, you need **integration tests**.

Integration tests, as the name suggests, are about testing the integration of your application with that of others to see if the application you are testing behaves as expected when interacting with a different application. You can also use them to test how modules inside your application integrate with each other because ideally, you want to run your integration tests against a real running application. In the next session, we will show you how to run tests against a real, running Cargo Tracker application. To achieve this, we will use Testcontainers.

What is Testcontainers?

Testcontainers is a piece of software developed by AtomicJar. It is an open source framework that provides an abstraction around spinning up and breaking down Docker containers for testing purposes. It gives you an easy and lightweight interface through which you can manage your containers. There is also a library that makes integration with JUnit 5 very simple. With Testcontainers, you can do the following:

- More easily test our application more realistically.

- Test how your systems integrate with real dependencies instead of having to use mocks or stubs. For example, you can spin up a real database.

- Make sure your test environment is portable. Every user will spin up the same Docker containers, making it easy for everyone to start using and extending the integration tests.

- Prevent bugs from happening later during development. You can now test the integration before deploying to a development, test, or acceptance environment.

Setting up Testcontainers

To start using Testcontainers, you need to have a few things set up. You need a valid Docker environment. Check out *Chapter 6*, on how to set up Docker on your machine if you haven't already. To add Testcontainers to your project, you need to add three dependencies.

We need the following dependencies to run the integration tests:

- JUnit 5

- Testcontainers

- Testcontainers JUnit integration

We need the JUnit 5 dependency to have something that can run the test you are going to create. The Testcontainers dependency is needed as an easy way to interact with Docker instances, and the Testcontainers JUnit integration is used to make the two earlier-mentioned dependencies work together. Adding these dependencies is very straightforward. You only need to add these dependencies to the pom.xml file of the project, as follows:

```
<dependency>
 <groupId>org.junit.jupiter</groupId>
 <artifactId>junit-jupiter</artifactId>
 <version>5.9.3</version>
 <scope>test</scope>
</dependency>
<dependency>
 <groupId>org.testcontainers</groupId>
 <artifactId>testcontainers</artifactId>
 <version>1.18.3</version>
 <scope>test</scope>
</dependency>
<dependency>
 <groupId>org.testcontainers</groupId>
 <artifactId>junit-jupiter</artifactId>
 <version>1.18.3</version>
 <scope>test</scope>
</dependency>
```

With these dependencies added, you can start creating integration tests with Testcontainers.

For the integration, we are going to start with an empty class that will hold the integration test we are going to create:

```
@Testcontainers
public class IntegrationTests {
}
```

The class is marked with the @Testcontainers annotation. This makes it clear for JUnit 5 that we want to extend the test with the use of testcontainers. It will make it possible to use other annotations from the Testcontainers dependency.

With the test class ready, we can continue with the setup needed for the Cargo Tracker container we want to spin up for the integration test. To create a runnable container, we need a compiled Cargo Tracker application. To create this, run the following command inside a console:

```
mvn compile
```

You see the following output if everything worked, and the code compiled:

```
[INFO] -------------------------------------------------------------
----------
[INFO] BUILD SUCCESS
[INFO] -------------------------------------------------------------
----------
[INFO] Total time:  0.679 s
[INFO] Finished at: 2023-07-02T11:18:58+02:00
[INFO] -------------------------------------------------------------
----------
```

The compiled project will be stored inside the target folder of the cargo-tracker directory. When you navigate to the target directory and open it, you will see multiple files and other directories, but we are only interested in the cargo-tracker.war file. This is the file that we will deploy inside a container as part of the integration tests.

The next step is to make this cargo-tracker.war file available for the deployment. To do this, we need to create an instance of a mountable file. Here's how we do that:

```
public class IntegrationTests {

static MountableFile warFile = MountableFile.forHostPath(
  Paths.get("target/cargo-tracker.war").toAbsolutePath(), 0777);
}
```

The next step is to create a container using a Docker image of Payara that we can use to deploy the .war file too:

```
@Testcontainers
public class IntegrationTests {

  static MountableFile warFile = MountableFile.forHostPath(
  Paths.get("target/cargo-tracker.war").toAbsolutePath(), 0777);
  @Container
  static GenericContainer CargoContainer =
  new GenericContainer("payara/server-full:6.2023.2-jdk17")
  .withCopyFileToContainer(warFile,
      "/opt/payara/deployments/cargo-tracker.war")
  .withExposedPorts(8080)
  .waitingFor(Wait.forHttp("/cargo-tracker"));

}
```

This GenericContainer class adds a lot of code. So, let's break down step by step what happens. The GenericContainer class is marked with the @Container annotation this makes JUnit responsible for the lifetime management of the container. Behind the scenes, JUnit will use Testcontainers to do this. JUnit will instruct the Testcontainers dependency on a per test case basis on what it needs to do.

The GenericContainer class is made static because we want to use the same container instance for every test. If we did not use a static class, a new container would be started for every test and the old one would be stopped. This could be handy for certain tests but also takes some time. It is better to reuse containers if you want to speed the tests up.

Creating the actual instance is the interesting bit of the code. When you look at the following example, you can see that four things happen:

```
new GenericContainer("payara/server-full:6.2023.2-jdk17")
  .withCopyFileToContainer(warFile,
      "/opt/payara/deployments/cargo-tracker.war")
  .withExposedPorts(8080)
  .waitingFor(Wait.forHttp("/cargo-tracker"));
```

On the first line, we tell Testcontainers on what image we want the container to be based. When we have a container, we want to copy the .war file to the container so that it can be deployed. We don't have to call a deploy commando because Payara will deploy anything that is inside the /opt/payara/deployments/ directory of the container. On *line 3*, we specify the port we want to have exposed—in this case, 8080. This is the default port and makes it possible for us to call the container from the outside.

The last part of the code is very important. It tells us when the container is ready for use. If we had not included this line, it would have been impossible to tell if the container was ready. This could cause errors when a test runs too early and cannot reach the Cargo Tracker application, making the test fail. To prevent tests from running too early, we can wait based on a condition. In the case of the Cargo Tracker application, we want to wait till the Payara server is running and the Cargo Tracker application has been deployed. To test if the Payara server is running, we can make an `http` request to the **Start** page of the Cargo Tracker application. If this request is successful, we know that the application is up and running and ready for your integration tests.

To check if creating the container and deploying the Cargo Tracker application all work you can add the following test to the class:

```
@Test
public void isDeployed(){
  Assertions.assertTrue(CargoContainer.isRunning());
}
```

This test will check if the container is running and succeeds if it does run. This is a good test, but it does not tell you anything useful about the working of the Cargo Tracker application. So, let us create an integration test that will test the Cargo Tracker application.

Creating an integration test

In the previous section, we set up a Docker container that will run the Cargo Tracker application. This container is managed by JUnit using Testcontainers. In the previous section, you only set up the container but without a real integration test. In this section, you are going to build an integration test we will make an `http` request to the test container.

To make a request to the container, we are going to use `rest-assured` library. `rest-assured` is a library that gives us tools to test and validate REST services inside our test cases. To add the `rest-assured` dependency to the project, you need to include the following code snippet to the `pom.xml` file of the Cargo Tracker application:

```
<dependency>
  <groupId>io.rest-assured</groupId>
  <artifactId>rest-assured</artifactId>
  <version>5.3.1</version>
  <scope>test</scope>
</dependency>
```

With this dependency included, we can start making REST calls from within our tests. The next step is to build the test case. Let's start with an empty case that looks like this:

```
@Test
public void verify(){
}
```

This test case is just a method that is marked with the @test annotation that tells JUnit 5 that this method contains a test it can run. Now, let's make a call to the test container using rest-assured. Add the following code to the testing method:

```
List<LinkedHashMap<String, Object>> cargoResult = given().get(String.
format("http://localhost:%d/cargo-tracker/rest/cargo",
 CargoContainer.getMappedPort(8080)))
 .then()
 .assertThat().statusCode(200)
 .and()
 .contentType(ContentType.JSON)
 .extract()
 .as(List.class);
```

This method does a lot. Let's go over it line by line and see what it does:

- The example starts with an assignment to cargoResult. This will be a reference to the body of the request that we want to use later for further testing.

- After the assignment, you can see that a GET request is created for the cargo endpoint of the Cargo Tracker application.

- When you look closely, you can see that we must create a URL using String.format to call the Cargo Tracker application that runs inside a container. That is because we don't know which outside port is mapped to the internal port 8080 that the Cargo Tracker application listens to.

To find out which port is mapped to the internal port 8080, we must retrieve the port from the CargoContainer instance we created in the previous section, as follows:

```
String.format("http://localhost:%d/cargo-tracker/rest/cargo",
 CargoContainer.getMappedPort(8080))
```

This is the same String.format instance as the one from the previous example. As you can see, we retrieve the correct port by calling this method: CargoContainer.getMappedPort(8080). This method returns the port number that is mapped to 8080. We must do this as Testcontainers automatically maps the internal port 8080 to an available port of the host. After String.format, we have a functional URL that we can use to call the test container.

After making the call, we want to verify if the result is what we expected it to be. To do this, we can use .then() and .assertThat(), as in the following example:

```
 .then()
 .assertThat().statusCode(200)
 .and()
 .contentType(ContentType.JSON)
```

In the previous code snippet, we do two assertions, as follows:

- The first assertion that we are doing is checking that the status code we get as a response is 200, which means the request was processed OK

- The second assertion we do is to check that the content of the response is JSON

The next thing we want to do is to retrieve the actual response that was returned by the Cargo Tracker application, the JSON that it generated. To do this, we can use the `extract()` method, which will use Jackson to convert the JSON to objects. In this case, we just want an array of string.

The following example shows you how to extract the JSON response from `rest-assured`:

```
.extract()
.as(List.class);
```

We can use the JSON response for further testing. We can use it for assertions on the size and assert if the content is what we expected it to be. You can see how this is done in the following example:

```
Assertions.assertEquals(4, cargoResult.size());

cargoResult.forEach(cargo -> {
  Assertions.assertEquals(cargo.size(), 7);
});
```

The complete integration test will look like this:

```
@Test
public void verify(){
  List<LinkedHashMap<String, Object>> cargoResult = given().get(String.
format("http://localhost:%d/cargo-tracker/rest/cargo",
  CargoContainer.getMappedPort(8080)))
  .then()
  .assertThat().statusCode(200)
  .and()
  .contentType(ContentType.JSON)
  .extract()
  .as(List.class);

  Assertions.assertEquals(4, cargoResult.size());

  cargoResult.forEach(cargo -> {
  Assertions.assertEquals(cargo.size(), 7);
  });
}
```

When this test is going to run, JUnit will spin up a container for the Cargo Tracker application and then perform the test when the Cargo Tracker application is deployed and reachable. When the container is ready, the test will run and make a call to the /cargo endpoint and verify the response from the Cargo Tracker application.

After completing this and the previous section, the complete testing method will look like the following example:

```
@Testcontainers
public class IntegrationTests {

  static MountableFile warFile = MountableFile.forHostPath(
  Paths.get("target/cargo-tracker.war").toAbsolutePath(), 0777);
  @Container
  static GenericContainer CargoContainer =
  new GenericContainer("payara/server-full:6.2023.2-jdk17")
  .withCopyFileToContainer(warFile,
      "/opt/payara/deployments/cargo-tracker.war")
  .withExposedPorts(8080)
  .waitingFor(Wait.forHttp("/cargo-tracker"));

  @Test
  public void isDeployed(){
  Assertions.assertTrue(CargoContainer.isRunning());
  }

  @Test
  public void verify(){
  List<LinkedHashMap<String, Object>> cargoResult = given().get(String.
format("http://localhost:%d/cargo-tracker/rest/cargo",
  CargoContainer.getMappedPort(8080)))
  .then()
  .assertThat().statusCode(200)
  .and()
  .contentType(ContentType.JSON)
  .extract()
  .as(List.class);

  Assertions.assertEquals(4, cargoResult.size());

  cargoResult.forEach(cargo -> {
  Assertions.assertEquals(cargo.size(), 7);
  });
  }
}
```

When you add this integration test to the Cargo Tracker application, you are ready to run the test. The result will be that the endpoint of the Cargo Tracker application is covered by an integration test. When a dependency of the Cargo Tracker application changes, you can run this test to verify that the endpoint still works as expected.

Summary

In this chapter, you learned about multiple libraries that are needed to create unit tests and integration tests for the Cargo Tracker application and your own projects. This is an important skill to have as it gives you confidence in your own code bases. Creating unit and integration tests are part of the day-to-day tasks of a professional developer.

In the first section of this chapter, you learned that unit tests are small tests that only cover the smallest unit of code. For Java, that is a single method. You created your first test from the ground up and made it run using JUnit.

In the second part of the chapter, you learned that integration tests cover the integration of internal and external dependencies. You created an integration using Testcontainers, which uses Docker and an image of the Cargo Tracker application for the integration tests. After setting up the test container of the Cargo Tracker application, we showed you how you can test this instance using `rest-assured` to make HTTP calls.

In the next chapter, we will take a closer look at how Docker and containers can be used with the Cargo Tracker application.

Part 3:

Embracing the Cloud

In this part, you will delve into transforming the Cargo Tracker application to seamlessly embrace the cloud. With the application now running on Jakarta 10, you will learn how to create an Docker container and run it on an Kubernetes cluster. Subsequently, you will learn the essence of cloud native and how to deploy an application on an Azure Cloud environment. This part ends with a chapter about MicroProfile as it helps Jakarta EE in becoming truly cloud-native.

This part has the following chapters:

- *Chapter 6, Introduction to Containers and Docker*
- *Chapter 7, Meet Kubernetes*
- *Chapter 8, What is Cloud Native*
- *Chapter 9, Deploying Jakarta EE Applications in the Cloud*
- *Chapter 10, Introducing MicroProfile*
- *Appendix A, Java EE to Jakarta EE names*
- *Appendix B, As a Service*

6

Introduction to Containers and Docker

In the previous chapter, you learned how to test the Cargo Tracker application. At this point, the Cargo Tracker application is ready to be deployed to different environments, machines, and the cloud.

However, how do you ensure the environment is ready for the Cargo Tracker and that it can run there? In this chapter, you will look at how to solve that problem using containers and Docker. We will start with what containers are, what they can do, and how to create them. When you have the specifications for your container ready, you will install Docker and create and run the container.

In this chapter, we will cover the following main topics:

- What are containers?
- A brief introduction to Docker
- Installing Docker
- Running a Docker container

By the end of the chapter, you will have a clear understanding of what containers are, and how to specify and create them. You will also create a container for the Cargo Tracker application that you can run on every machine with Docker.

Technical requirements

For this chapter, you need to have a Cargo Tracker application on your system and need the result of the Cargo Tracker application of either *Chapter 3, 4,* or *5*. To edit the Docker files, you can use any text editor of your choice. We will install Docker on a Linux machine. If you want to follow those instructions, you will also need a Linux machine or virtual machine. You can also follow the instructions on the Docker website: `https://docs.docker.com/engine/install/ubuntu/`.

What are containers?

Before we dive deep into what containers are, let us first look at how the landscape looked before we had containers and what problems they solved. Before containers, deploying applications was a more complex and time-consuming process. Applications were deployed to physical servers or virtual machines, and developers had to consider all the different operating systems, libraries, and other dependencies that their application needed and had to support them. To complicate things even further, this had to be done in different staging environments – for example, a development, testing, acceptance, or production environment.

This meant that the process of deploying software was often manual and error-prone. Developers had to manually configure and install the required libraries on each physical server or virtual machine. This led to inconsistencies between different environments and deployment failures, due to missing dependencies, configuration issues, and a mismatch in versions of the dependencies used.

Moreover, deploying software on physical servers could be expensive, as each server needed to be provisioned and maintained, and scaling up or down required additional hardware purchases and configuration.

Now that we know what the situation looks like if you don't use containers, let's see what a container is and how it solves these issues.

Containers are a technology to package and deploy applications in a portable but, most importantly, consistent way. A container is a standalone executable package that includes everything your application needs to run – the application itself, a runtime, dependencies, configuration, and system tools.

Containers provide a way to isolate and manage applications and their dependencies clearly and consistently, making it easier to run and deploy software to multiple different environments. This makes deployments more consistent and reduces the number of deployment failures that happen because of missing dependencies and missing configuration, problems that you will find as soon as you try to run them on your own machine.

Containers have become a really important and indispensable tool for software development and deployment. One popular container technology is Docker; in the next section, we will dive deeper into Docker, what it is, and how it runs the containers that we create.

How are containers created?

Containers are the end result, but how are they created? A container is made based on an image. An image is like a blueprint that tells Docker how to create a container. With an image, you can create any number of containers, and they will all be the same. Docker will use the image as instructions on how to assemble the container.

The wonderful thing about images is that you can base your image on that of another image. By using other images, you create layers. For the Cargo Tracker, we can do something like this:

- The bottom layer could be an image that installs a specific Linux distribution
- The second layer could install, for instance, a Payara server that we can use
- The last image would be our Cargo Tracker application

We would have three images on top of each other, each building on top of the previous one. This gives us great reusability because we can replace the last layer with any other application that we want to deploy on a Payara instance.

A brief introduction to Docker

Docker is a platform that allows developers to package their applications and dependencies into containers. Developers can use those containers to deploy software easily and consistently across different environments. Docker was created by Docker, Inc. and quickly gained popularity due to its many portability and consistency benefits.

Docker Engine is the core component of the Docker platform and is responsible for building and running the Docker containers. Docker Engine consists of three parts:

- The Docker daemon
- The Docker API
- The Docker client

The Docker daemon is a persistent process responsible for managing Docker objects such as images, containers, networks, and volumes. The Docker client is a command-line interface that allows users to interact with the Docker daemon and manage containers. The Docker API is an API that can be used to automate Docker operations and integrate Docker with other tools and applications.

To start using Docker, you need Docker Engine installed on your system. In the following section, we will install the Docker Desktop application, as it also offers a user interface to manage containers and images. To create a container, you will also need a text file with instructions for Docker Engine on how it should create your container, which can run on any system with a container engine.

At this point, we would like to point out that Docker is not the only container solution available. However, Docker did popularize container usage. In fact, you might argue that Docker Engine is the default container runtime currently. A container runtime is a piece of software capable of running a container. There are alternative container runtimes, such as containerd and runc. If you are searching for an alternative to the Docker Desktop application, we would advise you to take a look at Podman.

Installing Docker

In this section, we will install Docker on a Linux machine. The first step is to obtain a copy of Docker. You can download it from their site: `https://docs.docker.com/desktop/install/linux-install/#supported-platforms`. There, you can select the platform/distribution of Linux that you use. For the following examples, I will use the commands needed to install Docker on a machine with Fedora, but you should follow the instructions for your own platform.

The first step is to install the `dnf-plugins-core` package, which contains commands so that you can manage the DNF repositories. Run the following command to install this package:

```
sudo dnf -y install dnf-plugins-core
```

The next step is to add the Docker repo using the following command:

```
sudo dnf config-manager \
    --add-repo \
    https://download.docker.com/linux/fedora/docker-ce.repo
```

With the repository added, we will download and install the rpm package. You can find the latest version of the file in the installation instructions of your platform. You can also use the following URL to use the same version as us: `https://desktop.docker.com/linux/main/amd64/docker-desktop-4.17.0-x86_64.rpm?utm_source=docker&utm_medium=webreferral&utm_campaign=docs-driven-download-linux-amd64`. When you have the rpm package, install it on your system using the following command:

```
sudo dnf install ./docker-desktop-4.17.0-x86_64.rpm
```

During the installation, you will have to answer some questions; the first one is about the dependencies that will be downloaded, upgraded, and installed and whether you agree with these changes. To agree, press *Enter*.

The second question is about whether you want to import a GPG key for Docker; again, press *Enter* to accept the import. Now, the tool will be installed on your Fedora machine.

When the installation is complete, you will see the following result in the console:

```
    xclip-0.13-18.git11cba61.fc37.x86_64
    xorg-x11-proto-devel-2022.2-2.fc37.noarch
    xz-devel-5.4.1-1.fc37.x86_64
Complete!
```

When you see this, you have Docker installed on your system. There are two ways to start the Docker Desktop application. You can start it from the **Show applications** screen or you can run the following command to start Docker:

```
systemctl --user start docker-desktop
```

In some cases, it can be handy to know whether Docker is installed on a system and, if so, to know what version of it is running. To check the version of Docker on a system, run the following command:

```
docker version
```

This will show you lots of information about what version of Docker is running, but this line in the output is particularly interesting:

```
Server: Docker Desktop 4.17.0 (99724)
```

This line tells you that you are using Docker Desktop version 4.17.0 as the server for your Docker containers.

Running a Docker container

In this section, you will take the Cargo Tracker application, build a Docker file for it, and run it as a Docker container on your system. We will start by creating a Docker file that you can use. Using the Docker file, we will tell Docker Engine how to create the container for us and how we want to run it. With the container running, we will look at how to use the command-line interface to manage the container to see the logs generated by the Cargo Tracker application. The creation of this Docker file will be the starting point of our journey toward running the Cargo Tracker on Docker.

Creating a Docker container

The first step to run the Cargo Tracker on Docker Engine is to create a Docker file. The Docker file contains instructions for Docker Engine on how to create the container we want. Start by creating a file named Dockerfile in the root of the Cargo Tracker application. Inside the Docker file, you need to add the following two lines of code:

```
FROM payara/server-full:6.2023.2-jdk17

COPY target/cargo-tracker.war $DEPLOY_DIR
```

The first line of code specifies the parent image that we want to use. In this case, we have opted to build our Docker image on top of a full Payara server with version number 6.2023.2, which also has support for Java 17. This means that our Docker container will have all the necessary tools to run the Cargo Tracker application seamlessly.

The second line of code is a copy command. This command is used to copy the Cargo Tracker application's WAR file to a variable named $DEPLOY_DIR. The parent Docker image we have selected uses this variable to search for applications to deploy. Therefore, by placing a copy of the Cargo Tracker in this directory, we ensure that it will be deployed automatically once the container is created.

After creating the Docker file, the next step is to use it to tell Docker Engine how to create the container and how we want to run it. Once the container is up and running, we can use the command-line interface to manage it and view the logs generated by the Cargo Tracker application. This will enable us to monitor the application's performance and make any necessary adjustments to ensure that it runs smoothly.

Building a container

The next step is to tell Docker Engine to build the container we just specified using the Dockerfile. To create the container, we will use the Docker client, which is a command-line interface that lets you interact with the Docker daemon and manage containers. Using the terminal, navigate to the root of the Cargo Tracker application where you just created the Dockerfile. When inside the Cargo Tracker directory, perform the following command:

```
docker build -t cargo-tracker .
```

This tells Docker Engine to create a container for the Cargo Tracker application using the Dockerfile we created in the previous steps.

If this command executes successfully, you will see something in the console that looks like the following:

```
[+] Building 0.5s (7/7) FINISHED
=> [internal] load build definition from Dockerfile 0.0s
=> => transferring dockerfile: 90B 0.0s
=> [internal] load .dockerignore 0.0s
=> => transferring context: 2B 0.0s
=> [internal] load metadata for docker.io/payara/server-full:6.2023.2-
jdk17 0.4s
=> [internal] load build context 0.0s
=> => transferring context: 192B 0.0s
=> [1/2] FROM docker.io/payara/server-full:6.2023.2-jdk17@sha256:6b-
96c248d0e2cf18d6768883a2881389acfd743b13758b15572423373173813f    0.0s
=> CACHED [2/2] COPY target/cargo-tracker.war /opt/payara/deployments
0.0s
=> exporting to image 0.0s
=> => exporting layers 0.0s
=> => writing image sha256:7d7ff9b0a3290c692db4bb3f80b42d-
96203d67d312f3be0cf6c968b22a6913c5    0.0s
=> => naming to docker.io/library/cargo-tracker
```

This output tells you that an image has been created called `cargo-tracker` that you can use together with Docker.

Running a container

The next step is to run the Cargo Tracker application using the container we built in the previous step. To start the container, run the following command inside a terminal:

```
docker run -p 8080:8080 cargo-tracker
```

This command will start the container named cargo-tracker that we created in the previous step. The command consists of three parts:

- Run
- -p 8080:8080
- cargo-tracker

Run tells Docker Engine we want to start a container. Everything after the run is a parameter that will be passed to the Docker Engine. -p 8080:8080 tells Docker Engine that we want to map ports from inside a container to the outside. Without this, we won't be able to access the Payara server that we have running inside the container. The first 8080 is the port number on the host; the second 8080 is the port inside the container. Using this –p parameter, we can now use port 8080 to connect to the Payara server inside the container that is also running on port 8080. The last parameter, cargo-tracker, is the name of the container we created.

When you run the command, you will directly see the logging that happens inside the container. After a few seconds, you will something like the following in the console:

```
[#|2023-03-26T18:29:09.723+0000|INFO|Payara 6.2023.2||_ThreadID=216;_
ThreadName=Thread-24;_TimeMillis=1679855349723;_LevelValue=800;|
   SSLParams =org.glassfish.admin.mbeanserver.ssl.SSLParams@78a4a59b|#]
[#|2023-03-26T18:29:09.741+0000|INFO|Payara 6.2023.2|javax.
enterprise.system.jmx|_ThreadID=216;_ThreadName=Thread-24;_
TimeMillis=1679855349741;_LevelValue=800;_MessageID=NCLS-JMX-00025;|
SSLServerSocket /0.0.0.0:8686 and [SSL:
ServerSocket[addr=/0.0.0.0,localport=8686]] created|#]
[#|2023-03-26T18:29:09.802+0000|INFO|Payara 6.2023.2|javax.
enterprise.system.jmx|_ThreadID=216;_ThreadName=Thread-24;_
TimeMillis=1679855349802;_LevelValue=800;_MessageID=NCLS-JMX-00005;|
JMXStartupService has started JMXConnector on JMXService URL
service:jmx:rmi://0.0.0.0:8686/jndi/rmi://0.0.0.0:8686/jmxrmi|#]
```

This tells you that the Payara server has started and the Cargo Tracker application has been deployed. You can now access the server by going to the following URL: http://localhost:8080/cargo-tracker/. This is the same URL as when you locally run the Cargo Tracker application in a Payara server. However, instead of connecting to a local Payara server, you now connect to the Payara server inside the container.

When you click on the interface of the Cargo Tracker application, you will see the logging appear inside the console.

Running the container in detached mode

You can also run the container in detached mode using the following command:

```
docker run -p 8080:8080 cargo-tracker -d
```

Note that this command contains an extra parameter, -d. This parameter tells Docker Engine that we want to start the container in detached mode. When you start the container this way, you won't see the logging of the container. Instead, the command returns the container ID of the container you just started.

To see which containers you have running, you can use the following command:

```
docker ps
```

This will print something like this to the console:

```
CONTAINER
ID     IMAGE      COMMAND       CREATED       STATUS       PORTS        NAMES
c94fa6f7accf      cargo-tracker       "/tini -- /bin/sh -c…"       2
minutes ago      Up 2 minutes       4848/tcp, 8181/tcp, 9009/tcp,
0.0.0.0:8080->8080/tcp       inspiring_morse
```

This overview shows you the following:

- The container ID
- The image name
- The command
- The time the container was created
- The status of the container
- The port mappings
- The name of the container

When you run the container in detached mode, you can close the terminal, and the container will continue to run in the background.

Stopping a running container

If you want to stop the container, you can use the kill command and pass it as part of the container ID. The following example command kills a container with a container ID that starts with c:

```
docker kill c9
```

This command will print the ID you passed it when it has killed the container. In this case, the return value you will see in the console is the following:

```
C9
```

When the `kill` command has finished executing, you can run the `docker ps` command again, and note that there is no container running anymore. The output in the console will look like this:

```
$ docker ps
CONTAINER
ID      IMAGE      COMMAND      CREATED      STATUS      PORTS      NAMES
```

Using Docker Compose

Docker Compose is a powerful tool that is used to define and run multi-container Docker applications. It enables you to define the services, networks, and volumes required for an application in a single YAML file. This file defines the containers for each service, their configuration, and dependencies. We are especially interested in storing our configuration in this file. Doing so makes starting the container easier because we don't have to specify the container name or the ports we want to expose. We only have to define them once in `docker-compose.yml`.

Creating a Docker Compose file

To use Docker Compose, we need to create a `docker-compose.yml` file that Docker can use. Navigate to the root of the Cargo Tracker application and create a YAML file named `docker-compose.yml`. Make the `docker-compose.yml` look like the following:

```
version: "3.9"
services:
  cargo-tracker-app:
    build: .
    ports:
      - "4848:4848"
      - "8080:8080"
      - "8181:8181"
      - "9009:9009"
```

This is everything we need inside the `docker-compose.yml` file. This Docker Compose file creates a service called `cargo-tracker-app` that runs in a container and exposes its services on the specified ports.

On the first line, we define the version in which this Docker Compose file is written. This file uses version 3.9. The file defines a single service called `cargo-tracker-app`, which is built from the current directory (specified with `.`). The ports section defines the ports on which the container's services can be accessed. In this case, it maps the container's 4848, 8080, 8181, and 9009 ports to the corresponding ports on the host machine, making them accessible externally.

The build section indicates that the service will be built from the Dockerfile in the current directory. This means that Docker Compose will create an image for the container by running the docker build command, using the Dockerfile in the current directory.

Using Docker Compose

To start all the services in docker-compose.yml, run the following command:

```
docker compose up
```

This will build the container for the Cargo Tracker application using the Dockerfile in the current directory and starting it. Because we also specified the ports inside the Docker Compose file, we don't have to specify them in the command. When you see the following text in the console, you will know that the container has started and is ready to be accessed:

```
cargotracker-cargo-tracker-app-1  |    cargo-tracker was successfully
deployed in 9,380 milliseconds. |#]
```

You can now go to the following URL and see that the container and the Cargo Tracker application are running: http://localhost:8080/cargo-tracker/.

To see that all the ports are mapped to their corresponding port on the host machine, run the following command:

```
docker ps
```

The result will look like this:

```
CONTAINER
ID   IMAGE        COMMAND       CREATED      STATUS      PORTS       NAMES
93a1813c884c      cargotracker-cargo-tracker-app      "/tini -- /bin/sh
-c..."      30 minutes ago      Up 14 seconds      0.0.0.0:4848->4848/tcp,
0.0.0.0:8080->8080/tcp, 0.0.0.0:8181->8181/tcp, 0.0.0.0:9009->9009/
tcp    cargotracker-cargo-tracker-app-1
```

Under the port section, you can verify that the ports are mapped in the same we as we have specified in the docker-compose.yml file.

Stopping a container

Stopping a container that you started works the same as stopping any other container that runs inside Docker. Using the docker kill command, you can stop the container you started using docker compose up. To stop the container from the previous example, you can use the following command:

```
docker kill 93
```

This will return 93 and the container will stop. To verify that the command has worked, you can run the docker ps command again. Alternatively, you can use the following:

```
Docker-compose down
```

This will remove the container, the networks defined in the configuration file, and any default network definition.

Summary

In this chapter, you learned what Docker is and how you can use it for the Cargo Tracker application. You learned that a container is an executable package of your software that contains an application, dependencies, and the system tools your application needs to run. After that, we investigated what Docker is and how it uses containers. With this knowledge, you specified your first Dockerfile for the Cargo Tracker application. Using the Docker command-line interface, you have learned how to build your container and start it. You also explored other ways of starting the container using detached mode and how to stop a container. Finally, you learned how to create a Docker Compose file and how to start it.

These steps are very important for when we run the Cargo Tracker application in the cloud in the ·following chapters.

7
Meet Kubernetes

In this chapter, we will introduce you to Kubernetes. If you are already familiar with this technology, feel free to skip this chapter. If you are still with us for the ride, get ready to cover the following topics:

- The history of Kubernetes
- Why would you need Kubernetes?
- The key features of Kubernetes
- The architecture of Kubernetes
- Where to run Kubernetes
- Example of using Kubernetes

At the end of this chapter, you will have a good idea of what container orchestration systems such as Kubernetes do, how they work, and how you can utilize them yourself.

Technical requirements

This chapter does not have any technical requirements. If you would like to play around with Kubernetes, then here are some projects you could give a try. Minikube is a project that installs a one-node cluster on your local machine. Another project is **Kubernetes in Docker** (**KinD**), which starts a set of containers that will start Kubernetes. While these options can give you a good impression of what Kubernetes is and how it works, if you want to do some serious investigations, you might want to consider a cloud provider option. There are many offerings, such as AKS from Azure, GKE from Google, and EKS from Amazon. An interesting alternative is K3S from Civo, which uses cheap hardware to run Kubernetes.

We will perform a simple deployment to Kubernetes via a locally installed Minikube at the end of this chapter.

By the end of this chapter, you should have a good understanding of the position of Kubernetes within a cloud-native landscape. You will also have learned what functionality Kubernetes offers.

In the beginning

If you work in development or infrastructure in the IT industry, you have likely heard the name *Kubernetes*. It arrived on the scene in 2015, some eight years before we wrote this book.

Kubernetes started as a project in Google. Google is known for being a company that has embraced the cloud completely. All its products are cloud-focused. Just think about Gmail, possibly the most used cloud-based email product, and products such as Google Documents, Google Drive, and YouTube.

All of Google's services run in containers. In an article at InfoQ from 2014, it was estimated that Google starts 2 billion containers a week. That means more than 3.300 containers every second. With these enormous numbers, it is no surprise that there is excellent expert knowledge about running and managing containers.

Internally, Google uses a system that is named Borg, aptly named after the alien group from *Star Trek* that assimilates everything into one central hive.

Kubernetes itself is not based on Borg. Kubernetes, for instance, is written in Google's own programming language, Golang, whereas Borg is written in C++.

Yet, the core developers of Kubernetes have a strong knowledge of Borg, and many concepts of Borg are transferred to Kubernetes.

What is container orchestration?

In *Chapter 6*, you were introduced to Docker. You learned that Docker is a way of building and packaging software, allowing for easier distribution and execution. You also learned in the chapter about Jakarta EE and that it has introduced a specialized profile, the Core Profile, targeted at microservices and containerization. You are likely to have many containers running, and this is where container orchestration comes into play.

Container orchestration is the process of creating, scheduling, scaling, and monitoring containers. The number of containers that are required to run an application can quickly grow, even a standard architecture with a frontend, backend, and database – that is already three containers. And then you have additional requirements, such as a caching instance, a reversed proxy, and a CDN (`https://en.wikipedia.org/wiki/Content_delivery_network`) server.

Also, you might want to have more than one instance of each, in case of failure. As you can see, it is quickly growing. And if we throw microservices into the mix, where both the frontend and backend will be split into multiple services, the picture becomes clear.

It is no longer realistic to handle all these containers by hand – monitoring their running state and restarting failing ones.

This is where container orchestrators come in – they automate these tasks as much as possible. Note that Kubernetes is not the only container orchestrator, nor is it the first. Alternatives include Apache Mesos, HashiCorp's Nomad, and Docker Swarm. However, Kubernetes has become the de facto standard for container orchestration in the last few years.

Why would you need Kubernetes?

You might wonder at this point why you would need Kubernetes at all. However, even if your company is not the size of Google, or you are not running zillions of containers in your production environment, container orchestration via Kubernetes is something you are going to need.

As it turns out, Kubernetes has some extremely useful features that make it appealing to even small companies. In the remainder of this chapter, we will discuss these features in more detail.

Self-healing

One of the most useful functions of Kubernetes is the ability to heal itself. Should Kubernetes determine that a pod has crashed, then it will start a new pod to replace the failed one. That way, the cluster is brought back to the desired state again.

Of course, there are some constraints to this process. One of them is that there should be enough resources available to be able to start a new pod. Resources can refer to (virtualized) machines, memory, CPU, and storage capacity.

The self-healing capacity of Kubernetes comes into effect in two ways:

- It starts a new pod if an existing one crashed
- It kills a pod that is no longer processing user requests and is therefore no longer functional

Kubernetes has several ways to determine whether a pod is still functional, based on callback methods into the pod (liveness and readiness probes).

Another feature that shows the adaptive possibilities is the horizontal pod auto-scaling. If you think that this means that Kubernetes can scale the number of pods based on criteria, then you are right.

Horizontal pod auto-scaling works like this – if the load on a pod increases, Kubernetes will start an extra pod to relieve pressure from the already running pods.

If, at some point, the load on the pods decreases and we are still running more pods than originally configured, the auto-scaler will bring the number of pods down again. Of course, this is done carefully to prevent the remaining pods from becoming overloaded again.

Note that this process is called **horizontal auto scaling** because we start more resources of the same type, pods. If Kubernetes were to assign more CPU time or more memory to already running pods, it would be vertical scaling.

At fixed intervals, which currently default to 15 seconds (a value that is configurable), Kubernetes queries the resource utilization as specified in the auto-scaler resource definition.

This resource utilization can be based on a per-pod metric, a custom metric, or even an object or external metric.

Load-balancing and networking

Another area where Kubernetes shines is networking. Having to run many pods, each requiring its unique address, could easily mean that you have a lot of container ports to host port mappings.

Fortunately, Kubernetes takes care of this for you by assigning every pod a unique cluster-wide IP address.

This makes for instance service discovery a breeze; every pod can communicate with every other pod in the cluster. If a pod contains multiple containers, then all these containers share the same IP address. This means that each service can reach the other at the localhost address. It also means that each container in a node must have unique port numbers to avoid conflicts.

Kubernetes supports two forms of service discovery. Service discovery is the act in which one service needs to find and access different services to perform its actions. This could be as simple as the application needing to know what the database URL is to set up a JDBC connection.

Alternatively, it could be a situation where, for example, an Order Service needs to determine whether there is sufficient stock of a product for it to be placed in a shopping basket. Retrieving stock levels would be the responsibility of a different service – let's say, the StockService. The OrderService would need to know where (i.e., at what IP address) it can find the StockService.

The simplest mechanism that Kubernetes provides is via a set of environment variables that specify the hostname and port number for each service. In our example, the OrderService could simply look up these environment variables to determine the hostname and port number.

Furthermore, Kubernetes also supports DNS. If you have a DNS server set up in your cluster, then it will watch the Kubernetes API for new and removed services. This allows pods in the same cluster to find services based on their name.

Assume that we have a service that exposes a PostgreSQL database service and names it mydb. Other services can now reference this database service by this name instead of its IP and port combination. This gives tremendous flexibility and independence to your services.

Load balancing is supported in Kubernetes via so-called Ingress services. Ingress uses HTTP and HTTPS to make your services accessible from outside the cluster. It makes sense that, at some point, some part of your application should be accessible to the outside world, the world beyond your cluster. If we continue the OrderService example from before, to be able to add a product to a shopping basket, a user/buyer must have access to a website, for instance. This is where the ingress comes in. It can translate the external URL to a service running inside your Kubernetes cluster.

Load balancing is part of the Ingress functionality. There may be many pods that run the OrderService. Now, if a request comes in to add a product to the shopping cart, which service should it pick? Load balancing will take care of this problem by applying a certain strategy to picking the desired pod.

A few quite common strategies are as follows:

- Round-robin is one simple approach in which groups of pods are used in conjunction. On each request, the next pod from the pool is picked, each getting its turn.

- Another approach could be the fastest. In this scenario, the pod that is fastest in responding to requests is picked next.

- Again, a different approach could be smallest, meaning a group is created with just enough pods to handle the current load.

As you see, the possibilities are almost infinite, and so is the complexity. Often, the standard is good enough, and fine-tuning of load-balancers is only required once limits are reached.

Persistent storage and volumes

Containers, and pods, are ephemeral by nature. They are very often short-lived, and once they terminate, the data stored inside the pod is lost forever. It suddenly might sound a lot less appealing to store your valuable data in a database container, does it not?

The solution seems simple then – store your data outside of the container. This is exactly what Kubernetes allows you to do, and in doing so, it gives you an enormous amount of freedom and choices.

Kubernetes uses an abstraction called **volumes** to store data. In essence, volumes are just directories on a disk in which you store your data. We know two kinds of volumes, **ephemeral** and **persistent**, and you can mix and match them within a pod. Ephemeral volumes get deleted once the pod terminates, while persistent volumes keep existing beyond the lifetime of a pod.

Kubernetes supports many types of volumes, including some basic ones such as emptyPath, which is just a directory inside your pod that is empty when the pod starts. However, there are also several specific volumes, targeting the storage offerings of the major cloud providers. Kubernetes abstracts volumes away into a piece of configuration, which is called a **Persistent Volume** (**PV**). It describes the technical details of a volume.

Whenever a service requires some storage, it raises a **Persistent Volume Claim** (**PVC**). A PVC contains the requirements that a volume must meet. Think of things such as available size, type of storage, speed, and so on.

The role of Kubernetes in all of this is to find the appropriate PV to satisfy the PVCs. By abstracting things this way, a tight coupling between services and storage options is prevented.

As an example, assume that your application is currently using a PV of type azureDisk. Now, if, for some reason, you were to abandon this and switch to the GCE offering of a gcePersistentDisk, what would you need to change?

You would need to add a PV for the gcePersistentDisk, and you want to render the azureDisk PV unusable. However, on a restart of your application, it would state it needs a disk volume via an unmodified PVC, and Kubernetes would now attach the gcePersistentDisk PersistentVolume to your service. This is the power of abstraction that is found everywhere in Kubernetes, in pods, in volumes, and so on.

General

The basic idea of Kubernetes is surprisingly simple – the desired situation of your cluster is declaratively described and stored (soll-state). Kubernetes then executes a continuous loop in which it verifies the actual state of your cluster (ist-state).

If the actual state differs from the desired state, Kubernetes will take the appropriate actions against the actual state to make the two match again.

Pods versus containers

Kubernetes uses an abstraction over a container, which is called a **pod**. This is the smallest unit inside Kubernetes. You deploy, start, restart, stop, and un-deploy pods. You will never do anything in a container directly.

A pod can contain more than one container, the so-called multi-container pod. While this is a valid scenario, most Pods will contain only one container. Valid scenarios where you could have multiple containers in a pod would be a startup container, service meshes that use the sidecar pattern, and monitoring exporters. However, these are advanced concepts that go beyond the scope of this chapter. For more information, please visit: `https://kubernetes.io/blog/2015/06/the-distributed-system-toolkit-patterns/`

Some Kubernetes lingo

Earlier, we mentioned the phrase "cluster" without explicitly defining what we mean. We think it is a good moment to do that now.

We already said that a pod is the smallest deployment unit in Kubernetes and that one pod can contain a collection of containers.

Let us define some more Kubernetes terms:

- A pod is scheduled and executed on a node.
- A node is a worker machine in Kubernetes. It can be a physical or a virtual device.
- Worker nodes execute actual workloads.

- Nodes are controlled by the control plane. The control plane is the controller orchestration layer that exposes an API and manages all resources in Kubernetes.

- A group of nodes can be organized into a cluster.

- A service is a set of related pods that has the same set of functions.

Extending Kubernetes

Kubernetes offers an enormous amount of functionality out of the box, and its core is extended daily. Kubernetes has a large community of open source developers.

However, sometimes, Kubernetes might not have the functionality that you, your team, or your company require. What do you do? Should you dive into the source code? Fork the Kubernetes repository and add what you need to its core.

(Kubernetes is written in Golang, a programming language from Google. Unlike Java, Golang compiles to a native binary. A large number of open source projects that are part of the **CNCF (Cloud Native Computing Foundation)** (see `https://landscape.cncf.io/` for more details) use Golang – examples include Prometheus and InfluxDB. Uber is also known for writing much of its server code in Golang).

These solutions are not very sustainable of course; no one in their right mind would do that. (Although, some projects have done exactly that and still maintain sanity; K3S from Rancher is such a project.)

Kubernetes offers a very potent alternative, as you might have expected. We already mentioned that everything in Kubernetes is a resource and, as such, is described in a resource `.yaml` file. Pods, deployments, stateful sets, services, and PVs are all described in such YAML files. Kubernetes allows you to add your functionality to the core product in the form of Custom Resource Definitions. It is a contract that you need to implement, and then your resource will become a first-class citizen of Kubernetes.

This ability to extend Kubernetes but still be able to work with the standard product is one of the standout features in terms of maintainability. Instead of tinkering around in the core of Kubernetes and thus diverting from the main development, you stay in the main package.

Kubernetes architecture

The following is a diagram of the high configuration of Kubernetes. On the left, we can see the control plane, the part of Kubernetes that controls the scheduling, starting, and stopping of pods and services

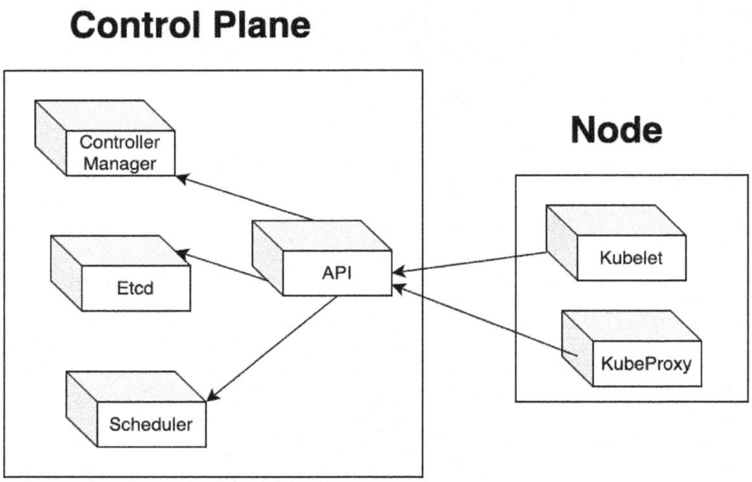

Control Plane

Figure 7.1 – The components that make up Kubernetes

The control plane has several components, which we will discuss in more detail in the subsections; they are as follows:

- The Kubernetes Controller is where the main control loop of the application runs. This is the place where the actual state is monitored and compared against the desired state of your cluster and changes to the cluster are being made if required. The Kubernetes controller contains a number of different controllers, such as the Node Controller, Job Controller, and ServiceAccount Controller.

- The Scheduler component watches over newly created pods that do not yet have a Node assigned to them. The Scheduler looks at the demands of the pod and tries to find a node that is suitable.

- Etcd is a distributed key/value store. This is where Kubernetes stores the configuration and state of the cluster. To achieve high availability, more instances of etcd are often active.

- API exposes the Kubernetes API that is both used by command-line tools (such as kubectl) and other front-facing tools.

On each Node, Kubernetes needs to have some software installed as well. These are as follows:

- Kubelet runs on each node and controls the containers that run on the pod

- KubeProxy runs on each node as well and oversees network-related tasks

What is not shown in the diagram is the **container runtime (CRI)**. Of course, to run containers, a container runtime should be installed on each node. CRI is an interface, and the following are supported:

- Cri-o
- Containerd
- Docker

In summary, this is the architecture of Kubernetes. As you can see, Kubernetes is not just one application. It is a collection of applications – some on the server, some on the clients – that cooperate to manage a potentially large set of containers.

Where to run Kubernetes

So, now that you know what Kubernetes is meant for and what functionality it provides (although we have only scratched the surface of this), the next question is, how do I run Kubernetes myself?

There are several options you can choose from if you want to run Kubernetes. Our list here is not exhaustive, simply because, almost daily, new options arrive. We will list the ones we feel are the most popular or most promising.

Use your own hardware

This might be the simplest way to start. Download and install Kubernetes on your own hardware. Depending on your needs, you might need quite a few computers. However, using virtualization on a few large servers might be enough to satisfy your hardware needs. Moreover, the smaller the number of computers, the lesser the cost of managing them is.

Keep in mind that this option still requires you to manage this cluster of computers and replace failing network interface cards and other broken hardware. You are also still responsible for backing up your data and monitoring the Kubernetes cluster. Also, let us not forget the need to apply software updates.

Still, if you already have an operations department in place that takes care of these tasks, and some hardware to spare, this might be a good option to start with. We recommend starting with the setup guide from the official documentation. There is also valuable information available about the demands of a Kubernetes production environment. As you will administer the cluster yourself, KubeAdm is the recommended tool to do this.

Using a hosted service

If you are into maintaining your own hardware and clusters, then using a cloud provider is a viable option. They can relieve the burden of providing hardware, administering the cluster, and performing operational tasks.

There are two scenarios here – you either use hardware from a cloud provider or a managed Kubernetes service.

When using hardware from a cloud provider, you are just leasing computer hardware. This can be either bare-bones hardware on which you must install everything or systems with an operating system preinstalled. The first option is called **Internet as a Service (IaaS)**, while the second one is called **Platform as a Service (PaaS)**. These are services that all cloud providers offer. It should be noted that IaaS/PaaS services include servers, networking, and storage.

When using managed Kubernetes services, the cloud provider has a managed Kubernetes cluster pre-installed for you to use. These services have become increasingly popular in recent years. There are several benefits when using such services. Authored security and simplified configuration come to mind, and also integrated monitoring and data backups.

Some examples of managed Kubernetes service providers are as follows:

- **Amazon Elastic Kubernetes Service (EKS)**
- **Azure Kubernetes Services (AKS)**
- **Google Kubernetes Engine (GKE)**
- **Digital Ocean Kubernetes (DOKS)**
- **VMware Tanzu Kubernetes Grid (TKG)**

This list is all but exhaustive; we leave it up to you to explore this in more detail, as prices and offerings may vary.

A simple example

In this section, we will deploy a simple Jakarta EE application to a local Kubernetes cluster To follow along, you need to have Kubernetes installed. The easiest way to install Kubernetes on your local machine is as follows:

- Minikube (`https://minikube.sigs.k8s.io/docs/start/`)
- KinD (`https://kind.sigs.k8s.io/docs/user/quick-start/#installation`)
- Docker Desktop (`https://docs.docker.com/desktop/`)

Following the link in any of the preceding bullets will bring you to the installation instructions for your tool of choice. In this example, we will use Minikube.

The application we will deploy is a simple Jakarta EE REST API. Once you hit the endpoint at `http://localhost:8080/api/greet`, it will welcome you with the famous greeting, "Hello, World!" If you would like a more personal approach, you can specify your name with a request parameter, such as `http://localhost:8080/api/greet?name=Packt`. The application will respond with `"Hello, Packt!"`

Below is the code of our simple webservice.

```
package com.packt.jakartaee.migration;

import javax.ws.rs.GET;
import javax.ws.rs.Path;
import javax.ws.rs.QueryParam;
import javax.ws.rs.core.Response;
 @Path("greet")
public class GreetingResource {
    @GET
    public Response sayHello(@QueryParam("name")String name) {
        String greeting = "Hello, " +
        (name == null ? " World" : name) + "!";
        return Response.ok(greeting).build();
    }
}
```

The application has been built, containerized, and uploaded to Docker Hub. It can be found at `https://hub.docker.com/r/ronveen/greeting`. You can pull the image via `docker pull ronveen/greeting:latest`, although there is no need for that – Kubernetes will take care of pulling the image for us.

Go to a terminal and enter the following command:

```
kubectl create deployment greeting --image=ronveen/greeting:1.0.0
```

As we learned earlier, kubectl is the command-line interface to the Kubernetes API. The create deployment command tells Kubernetes that we want it to create a new deployment for us. The deployment should be named `greeting`, and the container image to use is `ronveen/greeting:1.0.0`.

Wait a few seconds, and then enter in the command line the following:

```
Kubectl get deployments
```

You will get something like the following:

```
NAME        READY   UP-TO-DATE   AVAILABLE   AGE
greeting    1/1     1            1           12m
```

Figure 7.2 – Overview of the created deployment

You can verify that the deployment created a pod by entering this command:

```
kubectl get pods
```

```
NAME                        READY    STATUS     RESTARTS    AGE
greeting-5d5fcf847c-8jqt4   1/1      Running    0           14m
```

Figure 7.3 – Overview of the running pod

A pod with the same name as the deployment plus a unique suffix is created. At the same time, a service was created, which can be viewed by entering the following

```
kubectl get service.
```

The deployment is not exposed to your computer yet. For this, we need to expose it via the following:

```
kubectl port-forward service/greeting 8080:8080
```

This is best done in a new terminal window, as the port-forwarding will block the terminal from further input. We tell Kubernetes here that traffic arriving on port 8080 should be forwarded to the service named greeting on port 8080.

Now, when you open a browser and enter http://localhost:8080/api/greet?name=Packt you will see the following:

Hello, Packt!

Figure 7.4 – Output from our deployed application

Summary

In this chapter, we have given you a brief introduction to the origins of Kubernetes, why it might be useful to you, what its main functionality is, and what its architecture is.

It is highly likely that once you decide to migrate your code to a more modern cloud-native approach or start using containers, you will have to work with container management systems such as Kubernetes. This chapter has given you a good idea of how they work and where you can utilize them.

Kubernetes is the most downloaded product of CNCF. What exactly cloud-native is will be addressed in the next chapter.

8

What Is Cloud Native?

Understanding cloud-native principles is important as it will teach you how to migrate your legacy applications to a more modern application style.

In this chapter, we're going to introduce you to cloud native. We will explain what it is about and what its principles are.

We will discuss the following subjects:

- What is cloud native?
- Cloud-native principles
- Introducing the 12-factor app
- How to start the transformation

After completing this chapter, you will have a thorough understanding of what it means to develop cloud-native applications and what the requirements of those types of applications are. You will also be given some guidelines on how to start your own cloud-native journey with your applications.

Technical requirements

There are no prerequisites for this chapter, other than a healthy appetite for learning.

What is cloud native?

By now, you should be aware that modern applications depend on different methods of both software development and technology. The cloud is everywhere around us. You are likely to use cloud-based applications yourself. I am not only talking about email. Think of the many apps you have installed on your mobile phone. Most of them will use some kind of backend where application logic is executed to produce the results you want. A very recognizable example is the Amazon app, which allows you to order products from the convenience of your mobile phone. Your phone is just the frontend, the UI, to a very intelligent and diverse backend that runs in Amazon's own cloud.

But that is not all. Many of us use the cloud as a backup these days. It is very common to store photos on your phone not only on the device itself but also keep a copy for safekeeping in some kind of cloud storage. iCloud from Apple is a good example of this, but there are also other cloud storage providers such as Google Cloud and Dropbox.

Nowadays, there are many cloud providers, with **Amazon Web Services** (**AWS**), Microsoft Azure, and Google Cloud being the predominant ones. Perhaps less known in Western countries, Alibaba Cloud is the fourth largest cloud provider in the world, and its share in the cloud market is not that far off Google Cloud's. So, we can safely say that the cloud is everywhere these days.

Cloud native means that we are adapting our applications to the new possibilities offered by the cloud. We need to keep in mind, though, that the cloud is driven by a different set of architectural constraints. In the following sections, we will explain these constraints in a simple fashion.

Cloud-native principles

I am sure you have heard the words *cloud native* many times, even before picking up this book. Maybe hearing those words was what made you choose to read this book. Let us now carefully examine the principles of cloud native.

Cloud native is driven by four different features, which are as follows:

- Microservices
- Containers and orchestration
- DevOps
- **Continuous integration and continuous delivery (CI/CD)**

We will discuss each of these features in more detail in this chapter, but you have to realize we can only scratch the surface here. Each of them deserves a book in its own right, and in fact, you can find books from Packt Publishing on these subjects.

Microservices

While it is not a requirement to run microservices in the cloud, most cloud-native applications are in fact microservices. We have already come across the term *microservices* in the book a few times, but let's look at a definition first.

Microservices is an architectural style that structures an application as a collection of services that are as follows:

- Independently deployable
- Loosely coupled

- Organized around business capabilities
- Owned by a dedicated team

Independent deployability is of crucial importance. You should be able to deploy new or updated services into production without being concerned about disrupting other services or having to remember to redeploy these other services. This will be described in more detail in the *Introducing the 12-factor app* section of this chapter.

Loose coupling in software development is always a good idea, but even more so in microservices. It allows for services to change over time without these changes affecting other services. There are many things to consider in order to achieve loose coupling, but the most important ones are using distinct database schemas for each of your services, communicating via APIs (remember the quote from Jeff Bezos of Amazon on this: "*All service interfaces, without exception, must be designed from the ground up to be externalizable*"), and providing asynchronous communication between your services.

That these services should be organized around a business domain goes without saying: their sole reason for existence is that they in some way support the business process of the company that is utilizing them.

Finally, they should be owned by a small team. The reason for this is that these services only facilitate a small part of the complete business process. As such, the amount of domain logic that is required is also limited. Compare this to traditional application development where every developer had to potentially work on the entire application. This would require knowledge of the complete business domain.

Onboarding new members into your team becomes much easier and quicker with microservices. Also, changes to your microservices can be implemented much quicker as each developer knows all the details and the effect that these changes will have.

Containers and orchestration

In the chapters on Docker (*Chapter 6*) and Kubernetes (*Chapter 7*), we have already explained the advantages of using these technologies. In fact, you might argue that containerization is what made the cloud-native movement possible in the first place.

Creating artifacts, your application binaries, in an unmodifiable container that is pushed through the different stages of a pipeline (development, staging, production) has enormous advantages.

In systems consisting of dozens, hundreds, or even thousands of containers, some kind of container orchestration tool is a necessity. It also means that part of your operations will be automated, relieving the operations department of trivial work and allowing them to focus on more important and interesting tasks at hand.

DevOps

DevOps is a combination of **development** and **operations** into one seamless team. In traditional application development, the development department would create or update an application. This application would be unit tested and undergo acceptance testing. Once acceptance testing was done, the application would be handed over to the operations department.

Operations would execute the required operations to bring the application into the production environment, such as running database scripts or creating new application bindings.

Once running in production, if any bugs were discovered, the process of analyzing and potentially fixing them would also be the responsibility of the operations department.

In short, both teams worked in highly separated silos.

You will probably see that this is very inefficient. The developers, with all their knowledge of the intrinsics of the application, might actually be better suited to help analyze bugs.

Combining both departments into one seems like a logical move, where everyone in the team is responsible for the complete life cycle of the application, from development to running in production. This shared responsibility will inevitably create a stronger feeling of "owning a service" and will lead to more careful considerations when applying changes.

One of the key points of DevOps is that anything that can be automated should be automated, or as the adage goes: "*Automate everything!*".

CI/CD

CI/CD is a process where changes to a code base are automatically integrated into this code base and are rolled out to production.

CI works like this:

1. A developer works on a so-called feature branch to make changes to the system. A feature branch is essentially a copy of the original software (which is on the main branch).

2. When they are finished working on the task, they will run unit tests locally. Once these tests are all "green," meaning they all passed successfully, they will push the code to a **version control system** (**VCS**) such as Git.

3. An automation server will now start building the software that was changed. Once the build process is complete, automated tests will be run against the build. These will not only be unit tests but also integration tests.

4. If all these tests are successful as well, code changes made by the developer on the feature branch will be integrated into the main branch.

5. When a build fails, due to failing tests or because the **source code management (SCM)** system cannot integrate changes into the original application, the process will halt, and the developer will have to take action.

This process has several advantages. One is that the newly developed software on the feature branch is tested at an early stage to be compatible with the original software in the main branch. Any discrepancies will be discovered early, which means that fixing them should not take too long and will not be too risky.

Moreover, new changes will become available to other developers at an early stage, meaning that they will have fewer issues incorporating them into their changes. CI expands on CD. This is a process where, after the successful build in CI, the software will be automatically deployed to a staging environment or even the production environment.

Modern CI/CD pipelines have this process completely automated, some even so much that no human intervention is required to bring software changes into production.

This is achieved by highly automating all test efforts. These tests have to be so exhausting in their nature that the application can be deployed to production with a high level of certainty that it will function as per specification and is not likely to contain bugs.

From all of this, it might be clear that the whole CI/CD process is very automated. There are numerous CI and CI/CD servers out there.

Note that CI/CD can also be used outside of cloud-native development. In fact, it is very common these days for CI servers to be used in regular software development. What is mostly lacking is the CD part, as it requires a high level of automated testing. Next to that, often companies are not ready yet to accept that software is released into production automatically.

This might be the result of organizational procedures (in government organizations, it is very often still required that some **quality assurance (QA)** department has to give the final "go"). In other situations, companies can have a mental "blockage" of bringing software to production instantly: they still want to have a human eye and mind check out changes before they get released into production.

Introducing the 12-factor app

The 12-factor app is a description of how cloud-native applications should preferably be constructed. Initially proposed by the guys from Heroku, it has since become the de facto standard for cloud-native applications or **software-as-a-service (SaaS)**.

The most important aspect of these rules is that they can be applied in any programming language. In the following sections, we will walk through each of these 12 factors and highlight what makes them important:

- Code base
- Dependencies

- Config
- Backing services
- Build, release, run
- Processes
- Port binding
- Concurrency
- Disposability
- Dev/prod parity
- Logs
- Admin processes

Code base

One code base tracked in revision control, many deploys.

We already touched upon this before; there must be a central code base, stored in some kind of SCM system. Only sources should be kept here; binaries or other artifacts should be kept at a different location.

Nowadays, Git is the most used SCM system. It is a specialized form in that it is a distributed SCM system: developers store changes in their local repositories, which then synchronize with the central repository to merge their changes into the core.

A single code base is used to create a number of immutable versions of applications, which are put through different environments such as development, staging, and production.

Single code-based does not necessarily mean that all microservices should be placed in one repository, a so-called monorepo. While this model has become more popular through its use by big IT giants such as Google and Microsoft, it has its own problems.

The essential part of this factor is that all your code for one microservice should be in the same repository.

Dependencies

Explicitly declare and isolate dependencies.

Even if your microservice is of a very simple kind, it will still have some dependencies. This could be a library developed by your own organization, or a third-party library.

In a cloud-native world, microservices mostly know what their dependencies are. Often, multiple versions of these libraries exist, so having the exact version required is crucial.

Applications deployed on application servers rely on the server providing a certain set of shared libraries. Each application could then use these libraries without having to supply them itself.

While this may seem beneficial, it also violates our second factor stated here: applications should explicitly specify and use a specific version of a library. For this reason, a cloud-native application should never depend on shared libraries but should always be packaged with all the dependencies it requires.

In Java, we can use project configuration files in tools such as Maven and Gradle to explicitly state our dependencies and their versions.

Config

Store config in the environment.

Factor 3 states that applications should be configured by using environment variables only. This configuration data could be a URL and credentials for a database, or a secret key to use when accessing a different microservice.

These values most likely vary in development, staging, and production. By setting these values into environment variables, the application can retrieve and use them at application startup.

The application itself stays unchanged when it moves from staging to production, for instance, and only the environment variables will have different values, reflecting the configuration values of that environment.

Container and orchestration tools such as Docker, Podman, and Kubernetes offer very good support for working with environment variables.

It should be noted that environment variables are not meant for configuring application logic, such as the allowed number of retries of an invalid password. This kind of application-specific configuration should be stored in some kind of properties file or a database table.

Backing services

Treat backing services as attached resources.

Backing services should be treated as bounded resources. First of all, what is a backing service? A **backing service** is any external service that your application relies on for its normal operation. Think of things such as databases, messaging systems, and external services, but also disk storage. This last one might seem strange at first, but remember that we are running in containers. Containers are ephemeral by nature. This means that they are short-lived, and as soon as a container dies, any content stored inside that container is gone forever.

Bounded resources in this context mean that your application can state its need for a certain backing service, but it is the cloud runtime that is supplying the actual binding to this service.

Factor 3 states that configuration should be externalized, and this includes the actual backing services you will be bound to. This has the major asset that during runtime, you can actually change this binding. Thus, if some backing service is failing, the application can keep functioning by binding it to another resource—for instance, replacing a failing database server with a new one.

Build, release, run

Strictly separate build and run stages.

We already touched upon the need to automate our build process earlier in this chapter. Preferably, we use a build server to create an immutable instance of our application and package it into a container.

Releasing this artifact means giving it a unique ID of some kind. This can be some kind of a version number. Containers, for instance, allow you to add tags to them. One of these tags can be this version number. This will uniquely identify it from other containers.

The artifact will then be moved through the different stages—development, staging, production, and so on—without being modified.

The different environment variables applied in each environment will change its configuration accordingly. The artifact itself is not changed at any time. This will guarantee that if it was working in one stage, it would very likely do so in another stage as well.

Processes

Execute the app as one or more stateless processes.

Processes should be run as stateless processes and apply the **share-nothing** (**SN**) principle. This is a distributed architecture principle that states that no information is shared between nodes. This ensures that you do not create any **single point of failure** (**SPOF**) in your system.

Practically, this means that if your application caches data, it should do so by using a caching server as a backing service, and not cache data on its own. Caches take time to be populated and are best shared between similar nodes.

Traditionally, web servers had a notion of something called **sticky sessions**. This tied requests from a user to a certain server because this server kept certain information about the client session in memory, for the sake of speed.

Sticky servers violate SN principles and thus should be avoided. Similarly, sharing information between processes via data stored in files on a local disk should be avoided in all very simple situations. Uploading a file or image for processing is an example of such a situation.

Port binding

Export services via port bindings.

For traditional application servers or web servers, it is possible to have multiple applications running inside of them. (They are called (web) containers, not to be confused with containers in the Docker sense, which is the artifact that contains your entire application.)

Applications inside these servers would then be exposed by assigning a specific port to this application. This means that all of a sudden, the port number has become meaningful.

This approach is harmful to cloud-native applications in two ways. Running multiple applications in one container will reduce the ability to scale independently. It will also limit the ability to self-heal.

Assigning ports should be left to the cloud runtime, as it very likely already manages **service discovery** (**SD**), load balancing, and **fault tolerance** (**FT**) as well.

Exporting services via port bindings enables your services to act as bounded resources for backing services.

Concurrency

Scale out via the process model.

Traditionally, when applications hit their performance limits, the reaction would be to add more CPU, more memory, and more disk storage. This kind of scaling is called vertical scaling; the application becomes bigger.

Cloud-native apps developed with the 12-factor app in mind are stateless and share nothing. They are ideal candidates to scale horizontally (scale out). This means running more instances of the same application, instead of a single bigger one.

Scaling out via the process model means just that—running more instances of the application, hence running more processes.

This fits very well with the ability of cloud providers to supply an infinite number of nodes. We have already touched on the ability of **container management systems** (**CMSs**) to scale the number of running containers for an application based on the load that is placed on it.

It should be noted that some kind of vertical scaling is still an option, as cloud vendors will still allow you to choose between different types of nodes for your application, each one with its own CPU and memory size. But you only have this choice at the very beginning, for the first node. When scaling out, every next instance of your application will use the same type of node.

Disposability

Maximize robustness with fast startup and graceful shutdown.

Your application needs to start up quickly and be able to handle requests within seconds. Traditional application servers could take minutes to start. Nowadays, these times have improved significantly, but it is still not within the blink of an eye.

If your application is taking its time to initialize itself—for instance, by populating a cache or by executing some long-running processes, such as refreshing data via HTTP—the wait only becomes longer.

Caches should be external resources, and long-running actions should be done after startup.

In fact, long startup times might make the CMS assume that your application is malfunctioning, and it could decide to kill the application even before it gets a chance to start executing.

Similarly, your application should shut down quickly, while still remaining consistent. It should be resistant to hardware failure. A sudden shutdown should not result in data loss.

The ability to quickly start and stop is essential, as this is an indispensable feature of truly cloud-native applications.

Dev/prod parity

Keep development, staging, and production as similar as possible.

The idea behind this factor is to avoid the "works on my machine" situation, and instead provide the confidence that an application works in every environment.

There are three main areas of focus for this factor. We'll look at these next.

Time

In projects that used the waterfall project management methodology, it often took weeks to months before changes made it to production. This meant that remembering what exactly went to production might become difficult. Release notes can only tell so much. More importantly, the developer would have forgotten most of the details involved when moving to production.

Ideally, it should take days, hours, or even minutes before a change makes it into production. As mentioned earlier, the result of the successful execution of a CD pipeline run is an artifact that is fully tested and thus can be moved to production immediately.

People

In classic IT organizations, developers will develop and testers will do the testing. Then, the application is handed over to the operations department, which will bring the application into production.

From there on, bringing the application into a running state as well as monitoring the application once it runs is in their hands.

This factor suggests that DevOps is quintessential to running your cloud-native applications. Development and operations should have a shared responsibility for both the deployment and the runtime inspection of the application. This will not only lead to a quicker delivery but will also increase the responsibility for the application, as felt by those who are part of the team.

Resources

A developer machine might look very different from the actual production environment, not only because of the operating system but also because of the difference in external resources. Locally, the developer could use a different database engine, have a different messaging server, and so on. They could use a different **database management system** (**DBMS**), perhaps running a free version on this local machine while a paid version is running in production.

If resources used in development are not the same as in the actual production environment, it is feasible that incompatibilities could start to creep in. As such, it is apparent that development and production environments should be similar.

Logs

Treat logs as event streams.

Logs can come from a number of sources, and not just your application. They are typically time-ordered streams of the output of all running processes and backing services.

Your application should never worry about routing logs or where to store them. Instead, your application should just stream its log output to `stdout`.

During development, the developer can easily view the log stream in their console.

During staging and production, each process stream will be captured by the execution environment and routed to one or more final destinations. These final destinations are typically log collectors that will store the information in some form or structure that makes the data easy to retrieve and view in specialized logging tools, such as Splunk or Kibana.

Admin processes

Run admin/management tasks as one-off processes.

Administrative tasks can be a number of things, such as—for instance—database maintenance tasks, some cleanup process that needs to be run on a regular basis, or, in general, cron jobs.

So, in general, scheduled tasks are considered a bad idea. Now, here is where we might have a different opinion. Java offers a lot of support for timed jobs, such as `EJBTimerBean` or `ScheduledExecutor` timers. There is no reason to disallow the usage of these kinds of timers.

And there you have it! We have discussed each of the 12 factors for cloud-native applications. It might be a lot to take in, and you might think that your application is still far from achieving some or all of these goals. But the only way to change that is to start planning, coding, and deploying. If needed, take one step at a time; if possible, take more.

How to start the transformation

If you are coming from a monolithic architecture, breaking it down might be a huge undertaking. It is not an easy and certainly not a quick process. As an example, Uber, the company that offers rides at a fixed price, came from a monolithic architecture. The monolith was written in Python and had a single PostgreSQL database. That was back in 2014. It has since transformed into a microservices architecture spanning more than 4,500 individual services. This shows that transforming your application landscape is not an easy feat.

To begin, you should determine the boundaries of services within your monolith to be able to extract them. Thinking in terms of a traditional **enterprise resource planning** (ERP) system, you could think of sales, purchasing, order fulfillment, and so on.

Identify which of these services you would want to extract from the monolith and how they would interact with the monolith once extracted. Interacting could be within the request/response model or asynchronous, via messaging.

You could choose to first pick services that change most often or those that currently cause the most problems. Another choice could be to select those services that have a problematic scaling tendency. The Strangler pattern is a very well-known pattern for achieving this. By carefully and systematically extracting each identified from the monolith, in the end, it will become an empty shell that can be discarded.

Some companies might find that their monolith is just too large to refactor in such a way. Then, the Lego approach can be applied, in which only new features are built in microservices. This will create a hybrid structure in which the monolith and microservices continue to operate side by side. While this will not solve the current problems with the monolith, it does provide a way to further expand the application in the future.

Summary

In this chapter, we introduced you to the concepts of cloud native and its principles. Furthermore, we introduced you to the 12-factor app and discussed each of the 12 factors in more detail.

You should now have a fairly good understanding of what is required to build genuinely cloud-native applications. We hope that this information will be an inspiration and a springboard for you to start developing applications, or migrate existing ones, as truly cloud-native apps.

In the next chapter, we will move our Cargo Tracker application to the cloud.

9

Deploying Jakarta EE Applications in the Cloud

In the previous chapters, you learned what cloud native, Docker, and containers are. With what we learned in those chapters, we are going to deploy the Cargo Tracker application to a cloud environment.

In this chapter, we are going to set up a cloud environment where the Cargo Tracker application can run. To do this, we need to set up the cloud environment first. You will learn how to set up a container registry in the cloud to store Docker images of the Cargo Tracker application, how to create a container instance from an image, and how to see the metrics of a container.

In this chapter, we're going to cover the following main topics:

- Deploying to Azure
- Creating a container registry
- Creating a container instance
- Metrics of containers in the cloud

By the end of the chapter, you will have a fully functional Cargo Tracker application running in the cloud that you can access from your own machine.

Technical requirements

For this chapter, you need to have an Azure account. You can create an account at the following website: `https://azure.microsoft.com/en-us/free`. With this account, you will be able to follow along with the examples in this chapter. The account is needed to create a container registry and a container instance. You can follow along with this chapter to get a grasp of what is needed to deploy a Cargo Tracker container in a cloud environment, but we recommend that you create an account and get hands-on.

Deploying to Azure

Azure is a cloud computing platform and service offered by Microsoft. It provides a comprehensive set of cloud-based solutions for individuals and businesses to build, deploy, and manage applications and services. Azure leverages Microsoft's extensive global network of data centers to offer a wide range of computing resources, storage options, and networking capabilities.

In this section, we are going to cover how to deploy the Cargo Tracker application to the Azure cloud environment. To follow along with these steps, you need to have an Azure account. To deploy the application, we are going to create two kinds of resources inside the Azure environment: a container registry and a container instance. When creating the container instance, we will deploy the Cargo Tracker application to the cloud. In the next step, you will be able to access it from a local browser.

Creating a container registry

The first resource we are going to create is a container registry. A container registry is a resource where we can store and manage images we create. We will use the container registry to store the Docker images of the Cargo Tracker application. The first step is to log in to the Azure portal at `https://portal.azure.com/#home`. Once logged in, you'll see a screen like this:

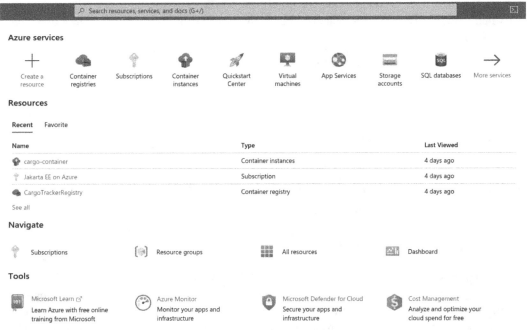

Figure 9.1 – Overview of the Azure portal

Use the **Search** bar at the top to search for the **Container registries** service:

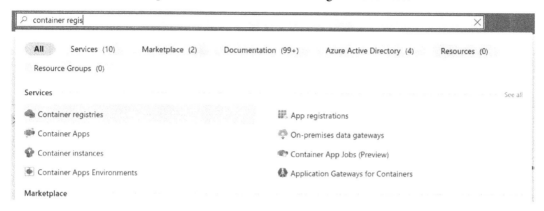

Figure 9.2 – Searching for the Container registries service

When you click on **Container registries**, you go to the **Container registries** service overview. This view will look very empty at the moment because we have not created a registry yet. Let us create one now. You can do so by clicking on the **Create** button in the **Container registries** service view:

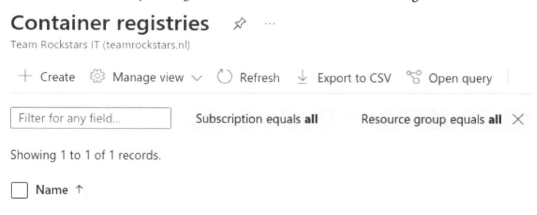

Figure 9.3 – Container registries overview

When you press the **Create** button, you will be sent to a series of forms you need to fill out to create a registry. In our case, it will look like this:

Create container registry ...

Basics   Networking   Encryption   Tags   Review + create

Azure Container Registry allows you to build, store, and manage container images and artifacts in a private registry for all types of container deployments. Use Azure container registries with your existing container development and deployment pipelines. Use Azure Container Registry Tasks to build container images in Azure on-demand, or automate builds triggered by source code updates, updates to a container's base image, or timers. Learn more

Project details

Subscription *	Jakarta EE on Azure ⌄
Resource group *	JakartaEE ⌄
	Create new

Instance details

Registry name *	CargoTrackerContainerRegistry ✓
	.azurecr.io
Location *	West Europe ⌄
Availability zones ⓘ	☐ Enabled
	ⓘ Availability zones are enabled on premium registries and in regions that support availability zones. Learn more
SKU * ⓘ	Basic ⌄

Figure 9.4 – Basics of the container registry

Here, we selected our current subscription and resource group. If you don't have a resource group already, you can create a new one. We chose `CargoTrackerContainerRegistry` as the name of the container registry. For the **Location** field, choose an option that is nearest to your location. For the **SKU** field, we chose the **Basic** option as we do not need the scaling performance of the **Standard** or **Premium** option. When everything is filled in, press the **Next: networking** button.

With the **Basic** SKU (service tiers) that we selected, we can't change the network connectivity setting. You can skip this step and go to **Encryption** by clicking the **Next: Encryption** button. In this view, we will again not change any of the settings because of the selected SKU, and can proceed to the next view by clicking the **Next: Tags** button. Inside this view, you can add tags. Tags can be extremely useful for grouping certain containers, but a tag is also something that is not mandatory, so you can proceed to the next view, which will let you review your registry and create it. Before you click the **Create** button, verify that everything is correct. The registry we will create and use throughout this chapter looks like this:

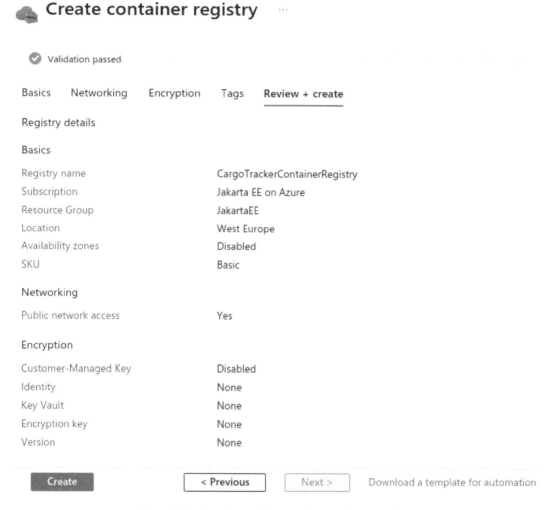

Create container registry ...

✅ Validation passed

Basics   Networking   Encryption   Tags   **Review + create**

Registry details

Basics

Registry name	CargoTrackerContainerRegistry
Subscription	Jakarta EE on Azure
Resource Group	JakartaEE
Location	West Europe
Availability zones	Disabled
SKU	Basic

Networking

Public network access	Yes

Encryption

Customer-Managed Key	Disabled
Identity	None
Key Vault	None
Encryption key	None
Version	None

[Create]   [< Previous]   [Next >]   Download a template for automation

Figure 9.5 – Overview of the container registry creation

If everything is correct, you can click the **Create** button. This will create a container registry for you in Azure. If everything is correct, you will see the following screen saying that the deployment of this new resource is complete:

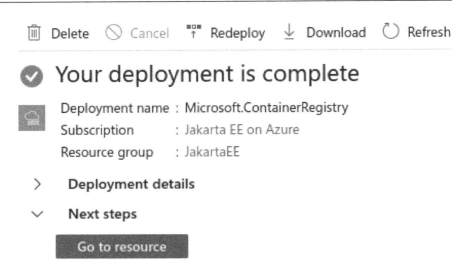

Figure 9.6 – Complete deployment of the container registry

Use the **Go to resource** button to go to your just-created container registry. This will show you an overview of the registry you created. For the **CargoTrackerContainerRegistry** container registry we created, this is how it looks:

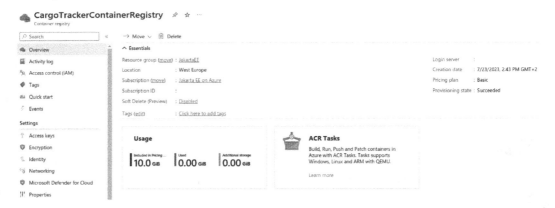

Figure 9.7 – Overview of the created CargoTrackerContainerRegistry container registry

Now the registry is created and ready, it is time to upload an image of the Cargo Tracker application to this registry. We will later use this image for the container instance that actually runs the Cargo Tracker application.

Uploading an image to the registry

We need to have an image before we can upload it. So, let's create one before we continue with the next steps, as follows:

1. Navigate to the directory of the Cargo Tracker application and run the following command:

   ```
   docker build . -t cargo-tracker
   ```

2. When you run this command, an image will be created of the Cargo Tracker application using the Dockerfile created in the previous chapter. The image will be tagged with the name cargo-tracker. Doing this makes the image ready for the next steps.

3. The next step is to upload the tagged image to the registry. To do this, we need two things: a registry and an image. To upload the image, you need to first log in to the registry. To do so, open a terminal and run the following command:

   ```
   docker login -u USERNAME -p YOURPASSWORD
   cargotrackercontainerregistry.azurecr.io
   ```

Don't forget to use your own password and username when running the previous command. When you run the previous command, you log in to the registry you created in the previous section.

1. The next step is to tag the Cargo Tracker image correctly. To do this, run the following command:

   ```
   docker tag cargo-tracker cargotrackercontainerregistry.azurecr.
   io/cargo-tracker
   ```

2. This will give a new tag to the cargo-tracker image. When you execute the previous command, the image is ready to be pushed to the registry. To push the image to the container registry in the Azure cloud environment, run the next command:

   ```
   docker push cargotrackercontainerregistry.azurecr.io/cargo-
   tracker
   ```

3. When you run this command, the image will be pushed to the registry. When you see the following output in the console, the image has been successfully pushed to the Cargo Tracker container registry:

   ```
   ~/Projects/Migrating-to-Cloud-Native-Technology-with-Jakarta-EE
   docker push cargotrackercontainerregistry.azurecr.io/cargo-
   tracker
   Using default tag: latest
   The push refers to repository [cargotrackercontainerregistry.
   azurecr.io/cargo-tracker]
   514967d1e96a: Pushed
   78ae8cbe633a: Pushed
   ade321fc98e5: Pushed
   cff05070dbef: Pushed
   ```

```
74b370e873af: Pushed
99413601f258: Pushed
a67a1a1c78da: Pushed
d543b8cad89e: Pushed
latest: digest: sha256:326a5f726e6b09a117d2a70649be00c35a3410d-
04fc1320464c853a93f358ce8 size: 2004
```

This means that the push was successful, so let's see if we can also view the image in the container registry itself. Using your browser, go to the **CargoTrackerContainerRegistry** service inside the Azure portal. Inside the left menu, you will see the **Repositories** service:

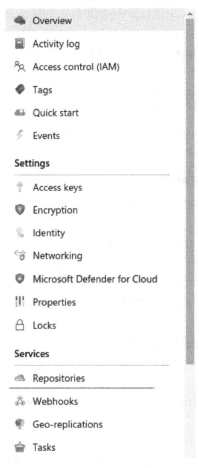

Figure 9.8 – Repositories menu item

Click on the **Repositories** button; this will navigate you to an overview of all available repositories. At the moment, this will only be the `cargo-tracker` repository, as you can see in the following screenshot:

Figure 9.9 – List of repositories

When you click on the `cargo-tracker` repository, you can see the image you just uploaded to this repository:

cargo-tracker ...
Repository

○ Refresh   ⌀ Manage deleted artifacts   🗑 Delete repository

∧ Essentials

Repository   : cargo-tracker   Tag count   : 1
Last updated date : 7/23/2023, 3:33 PM GMT+2   Manifest count : 1

⌕ Search to filter tags ...

Tags ↑↓	Digest ↑↓	Last modified
latest	sha256:326a5f726e6b09a117d2a70649be00c35a3410d04fc1320464c85...	7/23/2023, 3:33 PM GMT+2

Figure 9.10 – Latest image of the Cargo Tracker application

This rounds up the creation of the registry and uploading the image to the `cargo-tracker` registry. With all the preparation ready, the next step is to create a container instance that will use the `cargo-tracker` image.

Creating a container instance

In the previous section, you performed all the steps to eventually create a container instance in Azure. You created a container registry and an image and uploaded the image to a repository inside the registry. In this section, we are going to create a container instance that uses the uploaded image of the Cargo Tracker application. Using the **Search** bar at the top of the Azure portal, search for `container instances`:

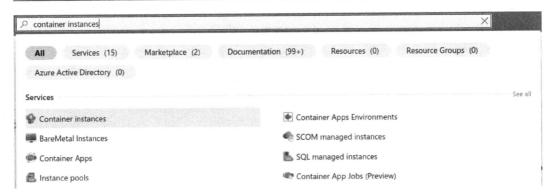

Figure 9.11 – Searching for container instances

Click on the selected result, **Container instances**, as this will bring you to the **Container instances** overview. Inside this overview, click on the **Create** button in the top-left corner of the overview screen. This will bring you to a series of forms that you need to fill out to create a container instance. It looks like this:

Create container instance   ...

Basics   Networking   Advanced   Tags   Review + create

Azure Container Instances (ACI) allows you to quickly and easily run containers on Azure without managing servers or having to learn new tools. ACI offers per-second billing to minimize the cost of running containers on the cloud.
Learn more about Azure Container Instances

Project details

Select the subscription to manage deployed resources and costs. Use resource groups like folders to organize and manage all your resources.

Subscription * ⓘ	Jakarta EE on Azure ⌄
└─ Resource group * ⓘ	JakartaEE ⌄
	Create new

Container details

Container name * ⓘ	cargo-tracker ⌄
Region * ⓘ	(Europe) West Europe ⌄
Availability zones (Preview) ⓘ	None ⌄
SKU	Standard ⌄
Image source * ⓘ	○ Quickstart images
	◉ Azure Container Registry
	○ Other registry
Run with Azure Spot discount ⓘ	☐
Registry * ⓘ	CargoTrackerContainerRegistry ⌄
Image * ⓘ	cargo-tracker ⌄
Image tag * ⓘ	latest ⌄
OS type	Linux
Size * ⓘ	1 vcpu, 1.5 GiB memory, 0 gpus
	Change size

Review + create   < Previous   Next : Networking >

Figure 9.12 – Overview of the basics of the container instance

You need to fill out the following sections:

- **Container name**: The name you want to give to the container
- **Image source**: Select the **Azure Container Registry** option

When you select this option, new fields will appear that you need to fill out, as follows:

- **Registry**: Select the name of the registry that you created in the previous section
- **Image**: The image of the registry that you want to deploy
- **Image tag**: The version of the image you want to deploy

Click the **Next: Networking** button to go to the networking step.

In this form, you need to fill out the following fields:

- **DNS name label**: This will be part of the **fully qualified domain name (FQDN)** of this container instance. For this example, we used `cargo-tracker`.
- **Ports**: Add port 8080 as this is the port the Cargo Tracker application listens on.

The result will look like this:

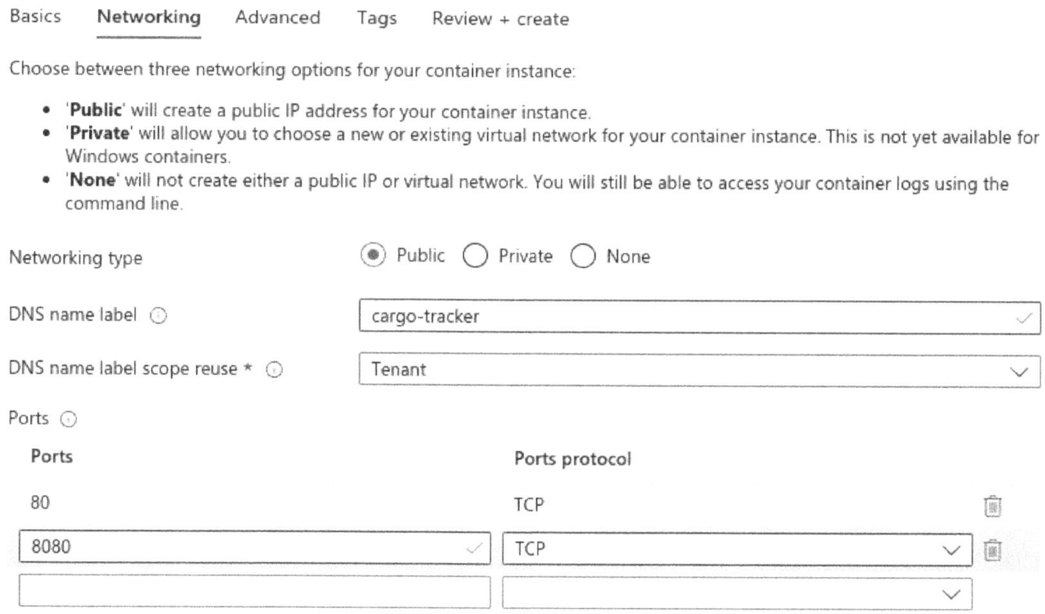

Basics   **Networking**   Advanced   Tags   Review + create

Choose between three networking options for your container instance:

- **'Public'** will create a public IP address for your container instance.
- **'Private'** will allow you to choose a new or existing virtual network for your container instance. This is not yet available for Windows containers.
- **'None'** will not create either a public IP or virtual network. You will still be able to access your container logs using the command line.

Networking type   ◉ Public   ○ Private   ○ None

DNS name label ⓘ   cargo-tracker

DNS name label scope reuse * ⓘ   Tenant

Ports ⓘ

Ports	Ports protocol	
80	TCP	🗑
8080	TCP	🗑

Figure 9.13 – Networking section of the container instance

Press the **Next: Advanced** button to proceed to the next step. We don't need to change anything in this form, so we can skip this step and go to the next step, **Tags**. The **Tags** step can also be skipped as we don't need to change anything in the form either. This will bring us to the last step: **Review + create**. Review this section to see if everything is correct. For the Cargo Tracker application we are building, it should look like this:

Figure 9.14 – Overview of the to-be-created container instance

If everything is correct, you can click the **Create** button, and the container will be deployed. When you navigate to the `cargo-container` instance overview, you can view information about the container, as shown in the following screenshot:

Figure 9.15 – Overview of the cargo-container instance running in the Azure cloud

As you can see from the **CPU** and **Memory** graphs, the container is up and running. Let's see if it works by going to the home page of the Cargo Tracker application that is running inside this container. To visit this container, we need to copy the FQDN from the overview that you can find on the right side. This FDQN is not enough; you also need to add this to the end of the FQDN: `:8080/cargo-tracker/`. We need to add this because the container is listening on port 8080 and the application itself listens to the `cargo-tracker` path. The complete URL will look something like this: http://cargo-tracker.g8gah7eecrcmbxcy. westeurope.azurecontainer.io:8080/cargo-tracker/. When you navigate to this URL, you will see the home page of the Cargo Tracker application, meaning that the container and application are running in the cloud:

Figure 9.16 – Home page of the Cargo Tracker application

FQDN is one of these typical abbreviations that you will find a lot in cloud computing. It pinpoints the exact location within the **Domain Name System (DNS)** by specifying the hostname, domain name, and top-level domain name. The top-level domain name for `www.packt.com` is `.com`, for example.

Metrics of containers in the cloud

One of the benefits of working in a cloud environment is that it comes with many functionalities out of the box. Next to automated backup and scaling, monitoring is another one.

In this section, we will briefly touch upon the monitoring capabilities that come standard with a cloud environment. The functionality shown here is specific to Microsoft Azure, but other cloud environments offer a similar functionality.

Once the container instance has been started, you have the option to look at its metrics.

To do so, select the **Metrics** option under the **Monitoring** heading on the menu bar at the left. You should then see a screen like this:

Figure 9.17 – Overview of container metrics

This view shows the basic metrics for an application—its CPU usage, the amount of memory used, and the number of bytes sent and received over the network. These metrics are always available, and rightfully so, because they are the primary indicators of how much load your application is experiencing. As such, they are the ones on which you may decide to scale your application, either manually or—more likely—automatically.

One of the interesting options is that if you hover over a metric, the timelines in all the other metrics change as well. If, for instance, you move your mouse to a spike in the **CPU** metric window, the **Memory** metric window will move to the same moment in time. This is extremely useful in comparing different metrics at a moment of some occurrence in the system:

Figure 9.18 – Overview of container instance metrics

When you click on a metric, you get a detailed view, and you are also able to switch between the different types of charts that are available:

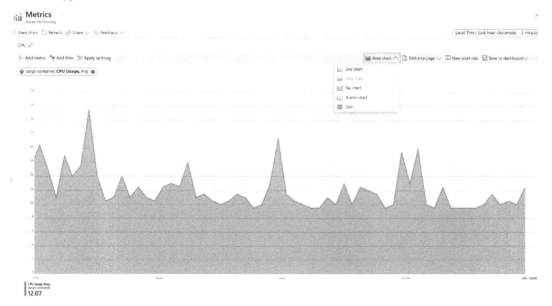

Figure 9.19 – Detailed view of a metric with the option to switch chart type

In the same menu where you can change the chart type, you also have the ability to set up an alert. Alerting allows for a certain action to be taken in case some predefined threshold on a metric is exceeded.

Here, we show the screen that is shown when you create a new alert:

Figure 9.20 – Setting up an alert

We selected a CPU-based alert, stating that the alert should fire if the average CPU usage exceeds 85. We also stated that we want this alert to be checked every 5 minutes and that it also should look at the last 5 minutes to determine the value. Normally, you would want this period to be a bit longer to get a responsible idea about the application load and to prevent alert firing due to an incidental spike.

Having a number of these metrics on a dedicated dashboard for a container instance can be very useful, and luckily, we have the option to do so. Via the **Save to dashboard** option, you can add your favorite metrics to your personal or shared dashboard.

Summary

In this chapter, we moved our application to a cloud platform. We chose Microsoft Azure, but it could have been any cloud provider. We showed how to set up a container registry, how to do the actual deployment, and how to look at metrics for a running container instance.

You have now moved your existing monolithic application to the cloud. You have enhanced it with cloud-native features, such as resilience. You have come a long way, and maybe this is where you intend to stop. Or, you may choose to go down the path of breaking up the monolith into individual applications or microservices. There is no good or bad here, and the choice of what to do depends entirely upon the application and its intended use. In the next chapter, we will look at MicroProfile as it can help add more cloud nativeness to your application.

10

Introducing MicroProfile

At this point, you should have a good idea of how you can move your application to the cloud. Even though your application is now running in the cloud, it does not mean that it displays. To achieve that, some extra steps need to happen. These extra steps can be made by utilizing MicroProfile.

In this chapter, we're going to cover the following topics:

- A brief history of MicroProfile
- What a MicroProfile consists of
- Looking at the core APIs in MicroProfile

By completing this chapter, you will have a thorough understanding of what cloud-native behavior is and how MicroProfile can help you add this kind of behavior to your applications.

Technical requirements

MicroProfile consists of several APIs for various tasks. All you need to do to leverage this functionality is to choose a MicroProfile implementation and add dependencies. This involves adding dependencies to your `pom.xml` or `build.gradle` file. An example of this can be found in *Chapter 4*.

Note that there a multiple implementations of MicroProfile available. Some of these are integrated into a full Jakarta EE offering, while others can be used standalone. For a complete list of these implementations, we refer you to the MicroProfile website `https://microprofile.io/`.

A brief history of MicroProfile

In 2010, Java EE was having a challenging time. New releases took an exceptionally long time to be created. It took 40 months to get from Java EE 6 to Java EE 7. And Java EE 7 to EE 8 took a whopping 43 months. At the same time, the internet was a fast-moving place and the cloud offered new opportunities and challenges. Microservices were becoming the latest architecture craze, and Java EE did not offer a default adoption.

Java EE Application Server vendors felt the need to offer additional features to the developers of their platforms. Unfortunately, everyone did it in their own way. It seems like a paradox that the platform meant to offer a unified API was now causing multiple competing and incompatible implementations to be developed. Each had a unique API that was different from the others.

This mismatch was recognized by multiple vendors, and as the speed of the Java EE specification process could not be improved, they decided to create a new project under the Eclipse umbrella that would supply a specification a bring those required cloud-native functions that Java EE was lacking. This resulted in the birth of MicroProfile.

Talks began in September 2016, and by August 2017, the first release became available. MicroProfile consisted only of JAX-RS, JSON-P, and CDI. These were all existing Java EE APIs.

Soon after, Config was added, and in the next release, version 1.2, JWT, Fault Tolerance, Metrics, and Health Check were added. This release was released in January 2018, showing the swift release cycles. More and more features were added to MicroProfile, while some became optional. This meant that an implementor was not required to implement these and could still be certified as an implementation.

At the time of writing this book, MicroProfile 6.0 is the current release. The following is a chart showing all the features it has:

Figure 10.1 – Overview of MicroProfile's features

Something new regarding this release is that it no longer mentions the individual Jakarta EE APIs – it now relies on the Jakarta EE Core Profile.

In the following sections, we will cover the following topics in detail:

- Config
- Health
- Fault Tolerance

- Metrics

- Telemetry Tracing

The other specifications are not of great interest to our Cargo Tracker application, and we will only touch upon them briefly, for the sake of completeness.

MicroProfile Config

According to the 12-factor app document drawn up by the people at Heroku, an externalized application configuration is an essential part of being cloud-native. Think of a URL and the credentials to a database. In container environments, this is mostly achieved by setting environment variables.

MicroProfile Config is meant for this and supports a lot more configuration options than just environment variables.

It supports a hierarchy of locations to look for configuration values. Each of these locations has an ordinal value, and higher-valued locations take precedence over lower-valued ones.

These locations are called **ConfigSources**. Three `ConfigSources` are required by the standard:

- A property file, `META-INF/microprofile-config.properties` (100)

- Environment variables (300)

- System properties (400)

The number between brackets is the ordinal value, so system properties have the highest priority. Accessing these system properties in your code is simple. You can simply use CDI to have them injected into your beans. Here is an example:

```
@Inject
@ConfigProperty(name = "customerUrl")
String url;
```

This code will lead to MicroProfile looking through the different ConfigSources for a property called `customerUrl`. Once found, it will assign the value of the property to the URL file.

Should the property not be found, a `RuntimeException` error will be thrown at startup, preventing the application from running. This can be prevented by adding a default value, like this:

```
@Inject
@ConfigProperty(name = "company",     defaultValue="https://www.acme.
com/api/customers")
```

Another way to prevent startup exceptions is by using an optional instead, like this:

```
@Inject
@ConfigProperty(name = "customerUrl")
Optional<String> companyId;
```

When you must inject several related properties, the code quickly becomes cluttered with annotations. To keep it more readable, a more recent version of MicroProfile Config introduced @ConfigProperties.

Imagine that you have these properties:

```
server.url=/api
server.host=https://acme.com
server.port=443
```

You can now define a class and add @ConfigProperties, like this:

```
@ConfigProperties(prefix = "server")
@Dependent
public class ServerConfig {
    public int port;
    public String host;
    public String url;
}
```

Now, in the class where you want to inject these properties, you can simply add the following code:

```
@Inject
@ConfigProperties
ServerConfig config;
```

One more appealing feature of MicroProfile Config is the ability to define so-called Config Profiles. Imagine that we have the following set of files:

- `META-INF\microprofile-config.properties`
- `META-INF\microprofile-config-dev.properties`
- `META-INF\microprofile-config-prod.properties`
- `META-INF\microprofile-config-testing.properties`

Each of these files represents the settings for a specific environment, which are dev, prod, and testing in this situation. By setting a profile name via a system property, the system will load the settings from that specific profile on top of the default properties files.

So, when using `java -jar myapp.jar -Dmp.config.profile=testing`, it will first load the settings from `META-INF/microprofile-config.properties` and then from `META-INF/microprofile-config-testing.properties`. When a property is defined in both files, the latter will override the former.

MicroProfile Health

Health is a wonderful thing – not just for us humans, but also for our microservices. Once you have deployed your microservices, you want to check their temperature occasionally. Enter the Microprofile Health specification, which allows you to validate the health of your services at regular intervals.

It should be noted that, although this specification exposes an API, it is not meant for human consumption, but more for machine-to-machine. Think of a container management system such as Kubernetes that wants to inquire about the status of certain pods to determine if they are still functioning as expected.

Three sorts of health checks can be performed, as described in the following table:

Type	Annotation	Usage
Readiness	`@Readiness`	Determines if the application is ready to process requests
Liveness	`@Liveness`	Determines if the application is running
Startup	`@Startup`	Determines if the application is still starting up

Table 11.1 – Health check annotations

For a valid health check, your bean needs to implement the `HealthCheck` interface. This functional interface consists of the `call` method, which returns a `HealthCheckResponse` object.

`HealthCheckResponse` needs to return if a service is either *up* or *down*. It can also supply additional information, such as a name. Furthermore, it can hold more details on failing resources. This can be specified via the `withData` method.

Here is an example of a `HealthCheck` service:

```
@ApplicationScoped
@Readiness
@Liveness
@Startup
public class HealthService implements HealthCheck {
    @Override
    public HealthCheckResponse call() {
        return HealthCheckResponse.named("Project")
                .up()
                .withData("redis", "Not available")
```

```
                      .withData("postgres", "Available")
                      .build();
    }
}
```

There are several interesting features here:

1. The bean is @ApplicationScoped as you will typically only need one bean of this type for your application.

2. The bean implements the HealthCheck interface.

3. In the example, this bean takes care of Readiness, Liveness, and Startup. You could of course define three different beans each taking care of only one task.

4. The up() method signals that the service is working as expected. To signal a failing service, you would use the down() method instead.

5. The withData method supplies more information. There can be an unlimited number of these methods.

6. In the end, a HealthCheckResponse object is returned.

MicroProfile Health exposed an endpoint at http://www.acme.com::9080/health.

Here is an example of the preceding health service:

```
{
  "checks": [
    {
      "data": {
        "redis": "Available",
        "postgres": "Available"
      },
      "name": "Project",
      "status": "UP"
    }
  ],
  "status": "UP"
}
```

Here, we asked the health endpoint for the status of the microservice and it replied by stating it was "UP". We can also see that additional information was sent in the data element. Both databases that were used are online. Should any system this service relies on not be available, it could be added here. This can be very useful in quickly identifying and resolving issues.

MicroProfile Fault Tolerance

So, we have our service configured and we can check its health. The next step for a microservice to become cloud-native is adding some resilience. The service should be able to self-heal within certain limits.

There are six annotations available within MicroProfile Fault Tolerance that can help make your service more robust:

- `@Asynchronous`
- `@Retry`
- `@Timeout`
- `@Bulkhead`
- `@CircuitBreaker`
- `@Fallback`

It is good to know that these annotations can be added to both CDI beans and public methods within those beans. Under the hood, they are implemented via interceptors.

@Asynchronous

`@Asynchronous` adds, well, asynchronous behavior to the method it annotates. It wraps them into a method that returns `CompletableStage` on which the other fault tolerance annotation can be applied.

`@Asynchronous` allows your code to run concurrently. Let's have a look at an example:

```
@Inject

// is annoted with @Asynchronous
private CustomerDetailsService customerDetails;
@Inject
// is annoted with @Asynchronous
private CustomerSalesHistoryService customerSalesHistory;
public CompletionStage<Customer> retrieveCustomerAsynchronously() {


        CompletionStage<CustomerDetails> result1 = customerDetails.
getDetails(customerNo);
        CompletionStage<CustomerHistory> result2 =
customerSalesHistory.getHistory(customerNo)


    . . .
```

```
    }


@RequestScoped
public class CustomerDetailsService {

        @Retry
        @Asynchronous
        public CompletionStage<CustomerDetails> getDetails(String
customerNo) {
        var details = retrieveDetails(customerNo)
        return CompletableFuture.completedFuture(details);
        }
}
```

We define `CompletionStage` for retrieving customer information. It consists of two steps – retrieving generic customer information and retrieving the sales history of the customer. This information is then combined into one object, `CustomerDetails`, that is returned.

In the preceding example, `getDetails` from `CustomerDetailService` is annotated with `@Retry`. This implies that when the method invocation fails, it is retried.

Synchronicity is achieved by MicroProfile by intervening when the method is called. It intercepts the method call and schedules it to be executed later, probably on a different thread. It then returns `Future` or `CompletableStage`. But this is not the one that is returned from the method because it has not been executed yet. Sometime later, the method is executed, and it returns its result.

If `Future` is returned, the originally returned `Future` will be updated with this result. If it is `CompletableStage`, Fault Tolerance will wait for this `CompletableStage` to complete before it flags the originally returned `CompletableStage` as completed.

While `@Asynchronous` allows a method that returns `Future` to run asynchronously, it can only apply fault tolerance features to methods that return `CompletableStage`.

@Retry

This annotation allows you to gracefully handle temporary network glitches.

The `@Retry` method can be applied to a class or individual method of a bean to indicate that if the invocation of the method fails, it should be tried again. A maximum number of retries can be specified as well as a maximum duration to retry for.

The behavior is simple – if a method returns normally, nothing happens. If it throws an exception, the method will be invoked again if the exception can be cast to an exception, as mentioned in the `retryOn` parameter. On the other hand, if the exception can be cast to one mentioned in the `abortOn` parameter, no retry will be executed and the method will throw the exception to the caller.

Here's an example of the typical usage of `@Retry`:

```
@Retry(maxRetries = 5, maxDuration = 1000)
public List<Project> findAll()
```

@Timeout

`@Timeout` prevents us from having to wait on the execution of a method forever. The value and the time unit can be specified. If the timeout occurs, a `TimeoutException` error is thrown. `@Timeout` can be combined with other annotations mentioned here.

Here's an example of the typical usage of `@Timeout`:

```
@Timeout(500)
public List<Project> findAll()
```

@Bulkhead

`@Bulkhead` is used to prevent one fault in the system from cascading to other parts of the system and eventually taking down the entire application. Its name comes from the shipping industry, where the hulls of tankers are made of separate compartments. If the hull is breached, the compartments are closed, and only the affected compartments are flooded, not the complete hull, thus preventing the tankers from sinking.

There are two possible flavors – the semaphore approach and the thread pool isolation approach.

In the semaphore approach, we specify the maximum number of concurrent invocations of a method. Here's an example:

```
@Bulkhead(5)
public List<Project> findAll() {
```

This says that there may only be five concurrent invocations of the `findAll` method. If a sixth invocation arrives, it will fail immediately with a `BulkheadException` error.

In the thread pool approach, the annotation is the same, but it is used with the `@Asynchronous` annotation, like this:

```
@Bulkhead(5)
@Asynchronous
public Future<List<Project>> findAll()
```

This implies that only five threads from the thread pool are allowed to run this method concurrently. The next requests must wait in a waiting queue. When the waiting queue is full, a `BulkheadException` error is thrown.

By working with these limits, the complete thread pool can't be exhausted. Otherwise, at some point, all threads would likely be executing this slow-performing method and there would be no more threads available to service the normally functioning methods.

The number of threads and the size of the waiting queue can be configured.

@CircuitBreaker

`@CircuitBreaker` allows for a fail-fast scenario. If a certain component is not working properly, the circuit breaker will open and no more traffic will be sent to that component. A circuit break can be in one of three possible states:

- **Closed**: In this situation, requests are sent to the component
- **Open**: In this situation, any request will immediately lead to a `CircuitBreakerOpen-Exception` error
- **Half-open**: In this situation, the system is probing the component to see if runs without failure

Here is a scenario: the circuit breaker keeps a *failure ratio* for a rolling window of requests. Once the threshold failure ratio is passed, the circuit breaker will open. Any requests that are sent will immediately lead to a `CircuitBreakerOpenException` error. After a configurable delay, the circuit breaker moves into a half-open state. Then, it probes a configurable number of trial executions. If any of them fails, it moves into the open state again. If no errors are found during all the trial executions, the circuit breaker is closed again, and traffic will flow freely to the component again.

Here's a typical usage example of `@CircuitBreaker` with the default values specified:

```
@CircuitBreaker(delay = 5000, requestVolumeThreshold = 20,
failureRatio = 0.5, successThreshold = 1)
public List<Project> findAll() {
```

The rolling window of requests to examine is 20. If in these 20, a minimum of 10 (20 * 0.5) fail, the circuit breaker will open. After waiting 5,000 milliseconds, it will shift into the half-open state. If one request succeeds in this state, the circuit breaker will close again.

@Fallback

All the annotations we have seen so far have tried to stop a method from failing. But sometimes, that is just not possible. In those situations, instead of returning an error, you might want to return alternative data, such as an empty return value or possibly cached values. For those situations, the `@Fallback` annotation is available.

There are two possibilities – fallback handlers and fallback methods. The following code shows an example of a fallback method:

```
@Fallback(fallbackMethod = "backup")
public List<Project> findAll() {
    return persistence.getAll();
}


List<Project> backup() {
    return List.of();
}
```

It is important to note that fallback methods should take the same parameters and have the same return type as the methods on which they are annotated.

Final remarks

While all the annotations we've looked at can work in isolation, it is possible and even advisable to use them in conjunction. Have a look at this code example:

```
@Retry(maxRetries = 5, maxDuration = 1000)
@Bulkhead(5)
@Timeout(500)
@CircuitBreaker(delay = 5000, requestVolumeThreshold = 20,
failureRatio = 0.5, successThreshold = 1)
@Fallback(fallbackMethod = "backup")
public List<Project> findAll() {
```

The annotations work together like this:

1. On entry, a timer starts to run.

2. The semaphore is inspected to see if the method may be invoked.

3. The method is invoked.

4. If an exception is thrown, the circuit breaker registers it.

5. The retry will kick in and a new attempt will be made; start at *Step 2*.

6. Once the timeout kicks in or the retries have been used up, the fallback method is invoked.

MicroProfile Metrics

Our service has been configured, we can reason about its health, and we have resilience in place. The next thing we want to do is know how it performs. How many requests are handled, what is the longest execution time, and what is the average execution time? Questions like these can be asked, and answered, by MicroProfile Metrics.

Metrics is a vast area. In this section, we will only discuss the annotations that can be used. But know that you can define your own metrics programmatically.

Metrics offers a REST API that is, by specification, required to respond with metrics in Prometheus format. Optionally, implementations are allowed to respond in OpenMetrics format.

Metrics come in three scopes:

- **Base**: Spec-described metrics that vendors may supply
- **Vendor**: Vendor-specific metrics
- **Application**: Application-specific metrics

The four metric annotations are as follows:

- `@Counted`
- `@Gauge`
- `@Metrics`
- `@Timed`

@Counted

`@Counted` counts the invocations of the annotated object. It can be applied to methods, constructors, and types.

Here's an example:

```
@Counted(absolute = true)
public Project findById(String uid) {
```

@Gauge

`@Gauge` samples the values of the annotated object. It can only be applied to methods.

There is no default unit for gauges, so you need to provide one when you define the gauge. A gauge is typically a value that comes from the application. Examples include the total number of customers, the average order value, or the number of processed parcels.

Gauges expose the return value of the annotated method, like so:

```
@Gauge(name = "total_projecrs", tags={"projects"}, unit = MetricUnits.
NONE)
public Long getProjectCount()
```

@Metric

`@Metric` contains the metadata information when a metric is requested to be injected. It can be applied to fields and parameters.

When using this annotation, the implementation needs to inject the request metric into the field or parameter:

```
@Inject
@Metric(name = "total_projects")
Long projectCount;
```

The value of the gauge that we defined previously is injected into the `projectCount` field. This allows your code to directly act upon collected metrics.

@Timed

`@Timed` tracks the duration of the annotated object. It can be applied to methods, constructors, and types. It tracks how often the object was invoked and how long it took to complete.

Here's an example of its usage:

```
@POST
@Timed(name = "project_create_duration")
public Response post(Project project)
```

Telemetry Tracing

The telemetry specification is new in MicroProfile 6. Telemetry assembles information regarding the applications running in a microservice environment. This information can come from various sources, most notably logs, traces, and metrics.

MicroProfile already had a specification for tracing known as the Open Tracing specification. Replacing one with the other did cause some stir in the community, but in the end, the choice of OpenTelemetry makes sense. It is a CNCF-supported project (`https://www.cncf.io/projects/opentelemetry/`). Furthermore, it is vendor- and tool-agnostic and can be integrated with a broad number of open source and commercial projects.

MicroProfile uses the OpenTelemetry project to implement telemetry. In version 1.0 of the specification, logging, and metrics are considered out of scope and be implemented in any way that's desired.

There are various concepts to understand regarding distributed traces: first and foremost, your application is performing several tasks. Some may be internal, some might be related to an external entity, such as a database, and some might include calling other external services. A distributed trace keeps track of all the activities and their duration. In doing so, it is possible to paint a clear picture of the complete process, spanning multiple systems.

As an example, assume you have a system that verifies if someone subscribes to a newsletter of your company. You need to verify if the email address is not already registered. If it is a new subscriber, register them and ask for the mailing service to send them the latest newsletter.

The message would typically arrive via because your application has a Jakarta Message listener (component 1) in place that listens to a specific queue. Next, your application (component 2) will verify if the email is already enlisted via querying the database (component 3). Finally, if the email address is not known, your application may invoke the `SendNewsletter` service (component 4) to send the current issue of the newsletter to the new subscriber.

(Note that more likely, your application would have placed a Jakarta Message on another queue on which the `SendNewsletter` services listen, resulting in an even larger number of components being involved).

If you want to have a complete overview of this process in real life, you need a trace that spans all these systems, hence the name distributed tracing. A distributed trace records the paths a request takes as it propagates through multi-service architectures.

A distributed trace consists of several spans. A span is a unit of work or operation. In the preceding example, invoking each of the components should lead to a span being registered in the trace.

Telemetry can be implemented in any of the following instrumentation ways:

- Automatic instrumentation
- Manual instrumentation
- Agent instrumentation

Let's look at each of these possibilities.

Automatic instrumentation

Jakarta RESTful Web Services and MicroProfile REST clients automatically participate in distributed tracing. You do not have to make any code changes to achieve this.

Manual instrumentation

Manual instrumentation is the process where you add tracing abilities. There are two possible ways to achieve this – the first through annotation and the second through injecting trace objects into your Java code. Let's dive into these options in more detail.

The @withSpan annotation

Using this annotation on CDI managed bean allows you to create a new span and establish a relationship with the current trace. You can state which parameters should be recorded in the span by using the @spanAttribute attribute on the @withSpan annotation. Here's an example:

```
@ApplicationScoped
class SomeBean {
    @WithSpan
    void span() {
    }
    @WithSpan("name")
    void spanName() {
    }
    @WithSpan(kind = SpanKind.SERVER)
    void spanKind() {
    }
    @WithSpan
    void spanArgs(@SpanAttribute(value = "theArguments") String args)
{
    }
}
```

Injecting trace objects

Several trace objects can be injected into your code via the @Inject annotation:

- OpenTelemetry
- Tracer
- Span
- Baggage

Once injected, you can manipulate the different objects to add spans to your code. Here is an example of retrieving SpanBuilder from Tracer to add a new Span object to the trace:

```
public class SomeResource {
    @InjectTracer tracer;
```

```
    @GET
    @Path("/add")
    public Response addSpan() {
        Span span = tracer.spanBuilder("addSpan")
                .setSpanKind(SpanKind.INTERNAL)
  .setParent(Context.current().with(this.span))
                .setAttribute("identifier", UUID.randomUUID().
 toString())
                .startSpan();
        span.end();
        return Response.ok().build();
    }
}
```

Note that span.end() is needed when you're manually adding a span to the trace. Not doing so will result in the span not being added to the trace.

Agent instrumentation

Agent instrumentation allows you to attach a Java agent to your application by specifying a JAR file. By doing this, you can add tracing support for several popular Java frameworks and libraries.

A Java agent is attached to a JVM with javaagent arguments, like the one shown here, but its specification may vary depending on the server you use:

```
 -javaagent: opentelemetry-javaagent.jar
```

Other specifications

There are several other specifications that we will touch upon only briefly in this section. This is meant to give you a quick introduction to their functionality.

OpenAPI

This specification supplies a Java API for OpenAPI, a specification that allows developers to expose their API documentation.

It holds no less than 46 annotations that can be added to your code and allows you to completely describe your API, resources, parameters, and return values.

The following example has been taken from the official MicroProfile OpenAPI specification documentation:

```
@GET
@Path("/{username}")
```

```
@Operation(summary = "Get user by user name")
@APIResponse(description = "The user",
            content = @Content(mediaType = "application/json",
                               schema = @Schema(implementation =
User.class))),
@APIResponse(responseCode = "400", description = "User not found")
public Response getUserByName(
        @Parameter(description = "The name that needs to be fetched.
Use user1 for testing. ", required = true) @PathParam("username")
String username)
 {...}
```

RestClient

The MicroProfile RestClient supplies a type-safe approach for invoking a RESTful service over HTTP. This can be achieved by specifying an interface that holds the methods of the remote API you want to invoke, annotated with RESTful annotations.

Again, from the official documentation, here is an example interface:

```
@Path("/movies")
 public interface MovieReviewService {
     @GET
     Set<Movie> getAllMovies();
```

This interface is then used to create a client in this way:

```
URI apiUri = new URI("http://localhost:9080/movieReviewService");
MovieReviewService reviewSvc = RestClientBuilder.newBuilder()
            .baseUri(apiUri)
            .build(MovieReviewService.class);
Set<Review> reviews = reviewSvc.getAllMovies();
```

JSON Web Token Authentication

JSON Web Token (**JWT**) authentication is an authentication mechanism that's used to identify an authenticated user and their roles.

It is generated by the server after successful authentication and then sent over HTTP to other services that a system wants to access. Commonly, JWT is both encrypted and signed. The receiving system can verify the signer and decrypt the JWT.

This authentication and authorization system is typically used in a service-to-service environment where each service passes the JWT along.

Jakarta EE 10 Core Profile

This specification is new in MicroProfile 6.0. Before this, the core MicroProfile specification included Jakarta RESTful Web Services, Jakarta JSON Binding, Jakarta JSON Processing, Jakarta Dependency Injection, and Jakarta Annotations.

In MicroProfile 6.0, it was decided to add these specifications into an umbrella specification by adopting the Core Profile from Jakarta EE. This new core specification is lightweight yet powerful enough for both microservices and edge computing.

Summary

In this chapter, you learned what MicroProfile is all about. We walked through each of the required specifications. The specifications that are of interest when upgrading the Cargo Tracker application to a cloud-native version were discussed in great detail.

We will see the Config, Health, Fault Tolerance, and Metrics specification return in the next chapter when we upgrade the Cargo Tracker application.

Appendix A
Java EE to Jakarta EE names

When Java EE was transferred to the Eclipse Foundation and rebranded as Jakarta EE, the names of the underlying technologies had to be renamed as well to avoid legal issues. The following is a list of the old Java EE and new Jakarta EE names:

Java EE name	Jakarta EE name
Java Servlet	Jakarta Servlet
Java Server Faces	Jakarta Faces
Java API for WebSocket	Jakarta WebSocket
Concurrency Utilities for Java EE	Jakarta Concurrency
Interceptors	Jakarta Interceptors
Java Authentication SPI for Containers	Jakarta Authentication
Java Authorization Contract for Containers	Jakarta Authorization
Java EE Security API	Jakarta Security
Java Message	Jakarta Messaging
Java Persistence API	Jakarta Persistence
Java Transaction API	Jakarta Transaction
Batch Applications for the Java Platform	Jakarta Batch
JavaMail	Jakarta Mail
Java EE Connector Architecture	Jakarta Connectors
Common Annotations for the Java Platform	Jakarta Annotations
Java Beans Activation Framework	Jakarta Activation
Bean Validation	Jakarta Bean Validation

Expression Language	Jakarta Expression Language
Enterprise JavaBeans	Jakarta Enterprise Beans
Java Architecture for XML Binding	Jakarta XML Binding
Java API for JSON Binding	Jakarta JSON Binding
Java API for JSON Processing	Jakarta JSON Processing
JavaServer Pages	Jakarta Server Pages
Java API for XML-based Web Services	Jakarta XML Web Services
Java API for RESTful Web Services	Jakarta RESTful Web Services
Java Server Pages Standard Tag Library	Jakarta Standard Tag Library
Contexts and Dependency Injection for Java	Jakarta Contexts and Dependency Injection

Appendix B
As a Service

Cloud providers offer different kinds of services. SaaS, PaaS, and IaaS are some of the most popular/well-known cloud offerings:

- **Software as a service (SaaS):** This is software that you can access immediately. You don't have to install or maintain it yourself. This gets done for you automatically.

- **Platform as a service (PaaS):** You can complete environments that you can use like development tools, database management, operating systems, and so on. You can fully focus on building the application.

- **Infrastructure as a service (IaaS):** This offers computing, storage, and networking resources you can use. The cloud provider manages the infrastructure while you maintain the operating systems, development tools, and your application.

You are not restricted to using only one type of service, many companies use combined services to best fit their use cases.

Index

Symbols

A

B

Packtpub.com

Subscribe to our online digital library for full access to over 7,000 books and videos, as well as industry leading tools to help you plan your personal development and advance your career. For more information, please visit our website.

Why subscribe?

- Spend less time learning and more time coding with practical eBooks and Videos from over 4,000 industry professionals

- Improve your learning with Skill Plans built especially for you

- Get a free eBook or video every month

- Fully searchable for easy access to vital information

- Copy and paste, print, and bookmark content

Did you know that Packt offers eBook versions of every book published, with PDF and ePub files available? You can upgrade to the eBook version at packtpub.com and as a print book customer, you are entitled to a discount on the eBook copy. Get in touch with us at customercare@packtpub.com for more details.

At www.packtpub.com, you can also read a collection of free technical articles, sign up for a range of free newsletters, and receive exclusive discounts and offers on Packt books and eBooks.

Other Books You May Enjoy

If you enjoyed this book, you may be interested in these other books by Packt:

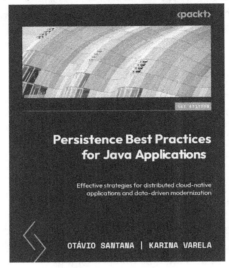

Persistence Best Practices for Java Applications

Otàvio Santana, Karina Varela

ISBN: 978-1-83763-127-8

- Gain insights into data integration in Java services and the inner workings of frameworks
- Apply data design patterns to create a more readable and maintainable design system
- Understand the impact of design patterns on program performance
- Explore the role of cloud-native technologies in modern application persistence
- Optimize database schema designs and leverage indexing strategies for improved performance
- Implement proven strategies to handle data storage, retrieval, and management efficiently

Practical Design Patterns for Java Developers

Miroslav Wengner

ISBN: 978-1-80461-467-9

- Understand the most common problems that can be solved using Java design patterns
- Uncover Java building elements, their usages, and concurrency possibilities
- Optimize a vehicle memory footprint with the Flyweight Pattern
- Explore one-to-many relations between instances with the observer pattern
- Discover how to route vehicle messages by using the visitor pattern
- Utilize and control vehicle resources with the thread-pool pattern
- Understand the penalties caused by anti-patterns in software design

Packt is searching for authors like you

If you're interested in becoming an author for Packt, please visit authors.packtpub.com and apply today. We have worked with thousands of developers and tech professionals, just like you, to help them share their insight with the global tech community. You can make a general application, apply for a specific hot topic that we are recruiting an author for, or submit your own idea.

Share Your Thoughts

Now you've finished *Cloud-Native Development and Migration to Jakarta EE*, we'd love to hear your thoughts! Scan the QR code below to go straight to the Amazon review page for this book and share your feedback or leave a review on the site that you purchased it from.

https://packt.link/r/1837639620

Your review is important to us and the tech community and will help us make sure we're delivering excellent quality content.

Download a free PDF copy of this book

Thanks for purchasing this book!

Do you like to read on the go but are unable to carry your print books everywhere?

Is your eBook purchase not compatible with the device of your choice?

Don't worry, now with every Packt book you get a DRM-free PDF version of that book at no cost.

Read anywhere, any place, on any device. Search, copy, and paste code from your favorite technical books directly into your application.

The perks don't stop there, you can get exclusive access to discounts, newsletters, and great free content in your inbox daily

Follow these simple steps to get the benefits:

1. Scan the QR code or visit the link below

https://packt.link/free-ebook/9781837639625

2. Submit your proof of purchase
3. That's it! We'll send your free PDF and other benefits to your email directly